FAMILY FOOTPRINTS

ଔଷ

A Memoir
by
Benjamin E. Potter

Family Footprints
Copyright 2015 by Benjamin E. Potter, M.D.
All Rights Reserved

As a work of remembrance, the author has set down names, dates, and other facts to the best of his recollection. The author has not in any way willfully misrepresented the past, and any errors should be construed as the small accidents that they are.

Published by Piscataqua Press
An imprint of RiverRun Bookstore
142 Fleet St. | Portsmouth, NH. | 03801

www.riverrunbookstore.com
www.piscataquapress.com

ISBN: 978-1-944393-01-4

Printed in the United States of America

Dedication to
Johanna Broughall Potter
and
Judith Harris Potter

Foreword

My purpose in gathering these family stories is to remember important and colorful ancestors. The Potters date back to 1638, when my father's side of the family, having sailed from England, first landed on James Island, near present-day Newport, Rhode Island. Mother's ancestors arrived from England in the late 1600s. Her father's family originated in Baden Baden, Bavaria, and arrived in America in the late 1800s. It is too easy to lose track of these relatives – a task made more complicated by the fact that our two branches of the Potter clan came together in 1923 when my mother, Helen Elizabeth Himmelsbach, granddaughter of the Rowland Potters of Bowdoinham, Maine, married my father, Milton Grosvenor Potter, in Buffalo, New York. Thus two Potter groups joined forces.

My children, and perhaps others in recent generations, have found our family history difficult to decipher. It is my hope that these notes will facilitate the perpetuation of our stories. In addition to stories of our ancestors, I have included recollections of my own life. I have been blessed with a great and close family. We are fortunate to have one another.

Enormous credit goes to Lorene H. Potter, official family genealogist, who with her husband, my brother, Grosvenor Potter, spent 10 years researching and recording our ancestors as far back as the 1500s. Lorene created an invaluable record of the Potter and Himmelsbach families by visiting numerous cemeteries, and church and town registries in England, Germany, and the U.S. Her work can be found in *Ancestors of Benjamin E. Potter* (1996). Another valuable resource is *A Genealogical and Biographical Record of a Line of Descendants from Nathaniel Potter of Portsmouth, Rhode Island,* by Irving White Potter.

I have been encouraged by my family, as well as by Norm Abelson, friend and former Associated Press correspondent, to continue recording family history and personal memories. While it has been difficult, due to my technological incompetence, I have continued the battle. Norm has indicated that, without a record of these stories, all memories may be lost. To be most interesting, he believes memories are to be preserved in a less chronological "duffle bag" style, rather than in a meticulous, "filing cabinet" fashion. I hope that present and future relatives will continue this process of documenting their own life stories for future generations to understand and enjoy.

Benjamin Elon Potter
Kittery Point
Maine, 2013

Table of Contents

A Brief Potter History	1
A Buffalo Beginning	5
Our Potter Grandparents: *Irving White Potter and Grace McDowell Potter*	9
Maternal Grandparents: *George Alexander Himmelsbach and* *Jeanette Potter Himmelsbach*	13
My Mother and Father: *Milton G. Potter and Helen Himmelsbach Potter*	17
Great Aunt Molly: *Mary Grosvenor Potter*	29
Moving About: The School Years *(1945-1949)*	33
At Sea for Two Summers *(1951-1952)*	37
A Broadband Trip through Europe: *1954*	41
Johanna Broughall Potter: *October 29, 1932-December 16, 1994*	45

Rotating Internship: Charity Hospital   53
New Orleans, Louisiana
(1957- 1958)

Deep South to True North   57
(1958-1962)

Wending towards Concord, New Hampshire   61
1962

Boundless "Banshee"   69

A Bright Light Ahead   77
Marriage to Judith Harris Potter
November 25, 1995

Brother Grove Potter Memories: 83
Notes from Westminster Church Funeral Service
Buffalo, New York

Retirement 101:   87
Kittery Point, Maine

Two Important People   89

Brother Paul Potters 70th Birthday Toast   95
January 23, 2003
Harvard Club
Boston, Massachusetts

Lobsters are the Bees Knees *A Talk with my McGill Medical School Class,* *50th Reunion* *Montreal, Canada*	99
Old Men and the Sea	103
The Mysterious Business of Mentoring Young Boys *in the Kittery, Maine Schools* *(2001-2008)*	109
Marvelous "Madrigal" Memories	113
Wrap Up	117
Afterword	119

A Brief Potter History
ಃ

My children, Heather Holmes McClelland, Benjamin Broughall Potter, and John Paul Potter are the three children of Johanna Blair (Broughall) Potter and Benjamin Elon Potter. Benjamin Broughall Potter, MD, represents the seventh consecutive generation of physicians on the paternal Potter side of the family. Dr. Benjamin Elon Potter, (1787-1826), the son of Jonathon Potter of Richmond, Rhode Island, was the first of this important line of physicians.

In 1638, Nathaniel Potter I (1617-1696), was the first descendent on my father's side of the family to land in this country. Nathaniel represented one of 14 separate branches of Potters to arrive in America from England. He settled in Aquidneck, which is now Newport Rhode Island. Nathaniel II, one of two children of Nathaniel and Dorothy Potter, was born in Portsmouth, Rhode Island. Nathaniel II and his wife, Elizabeth (Stokes) Potter (1638-1704), had 11 children. Nathaniel Potter III (1669-1736), and Joanna (Wilber) Potter (1668-1759) had two children, William and Mary Brownell Potter, born in Dartmouth, Massachusetts. These three Nathaniel Potters represent the origin of our paternal families, who all settled in Rhode Island.

William Sr. married Mary (Browning) Potter in Dartmouth. Their son, William Jr. (1715), married Elizabeth (Mosher) Potter, also of Dartmouth. One of William and Elizabeth's seven children was Jonathon Potter (1755-unknown). Jonathon and his wife also had seven children in Richmond, Rhode Island. Their second son, Benjamin Elon Potter, born May 10, 1787, would become the first Potter physician in our branch of the family. The family later moved to Jefferson County, New York.

Benjamin Elon married Phebe (Eastman) Potter on April 14, 1808. Phebe was the daughter of Dr. Hezekiah Eastman, son of Dr. Nathaniel Eastman. Phebe was related to George Eastman, who later founded the Eastman Kodak Company in Rochester, New York. Benjamin studied medicine at Rochester Medical School. Prior to the War of 1812, Dr. Benjamin E. Potter joined Dr. Nathaniel Eastman, his wife's uncle, in medical practice. Both doctor's had settled in a very sparsely populated area, the Holland Purchase, (now western New York State).

Seven children arrived in Benjamin and Phebe's family, including Milton Elon Potter, MD (1816-1875), my great-great grandfather, and the first Dr. Potter born in New York State. Dr. Benjamin E. Potter served as an army surgeon in the War of 1812. My son, Benjamin Broughall Potter, MD, has the original framed certificate, signed by the Lt. Governor of New York, naming Dr. Potter as the chief surgeon of his regiment. After the war, Benjamin had trouble supporting his children. His patients could not pay their bills. He was subsequently committed to the Poor House, and neighbors and relatives cared for his children until times improved. Nevertheless, Dr. Potter set out each day to visit his patients with horse and buggy, and returned to jail each evening. Benjamin died on March 30, 1826, at the age of 39, cause unknown. Phebe raised the family and died in 1874, at the age of 88. Both are buried in Attica, New York, near Buffalo.

Milton Elon Potter led a very productive life as a country doctor. He married three times. His first two wives died at ages 20 and 25, respectively. His second marriage, to Mary (Lobell) Potter, produced my great grandfather, Milton Grosvenor Potter, in Cowlesville, New York, on August 28, 1843. He was four years old when his mother died. Milton Elon Potter, a highly respected and skilled physician, died at home in Attica, New York, on November 1, 1875.

Dr. Milton Grosvenor Potter completed his medical training at the University of Rochester, but as a young man became professor of anatomy and dean of the Medical School at Buffalo. Dr. Potter, known for his lecturing ability, married Clara (Chase) Potter in 1866. My grandfather, Irving White Potter, was born on November 12, 1868; and Mary Grosvenor Potter, my great aunt and Irving's younger sister, arrived on November 1, 1871.

On January 28, 1878, at the age of 35, Milton Grosvenor Potter died at home (378 Virginia Street, Buffalo, New York). His two children, Irving and Mollie (Mary G.) were seven and five years old when their father died of tuberculosis, after two unsuccessful trips west in hopes of improved health. Milton's obituary describes a dynamic teacher, Dean of the University of Buffalo Medical School, and a very bright man, who was greatly missed by all who knew him.

The more recent Potter generations will be covered separately, but Lorene Potter's genealogy should be consulted for other specific dates and details. In studying these ancestors, I have come to wish I had known all these colorful characters.

Benjamin Potter

*Milton Elon Potter,
M.D., 1816-1875*

*Milton Grosvenor Potter,
M.D., 1843-1878*

A Buffalo Beginning
ଓଃ୨୦

I began life in this world on September 28, 1930, at the Millard Filmore Hospital in Buffalo, New York. My grandfather, Irving Potter, obstetrician, arrived to officiate following my mother's quick trip from the Canadian lakeshore where the family had been vacationing. Grandpa Potter had developed the internal podalic version method of birth, by which he turned the baby from a headfirst to a feet-first (breech) position. When he found me about to deliver in the old fashioned way, he was heard to say in a loud voice, "No grandchild of mine will be born head first!" He proceeded to turn me and deliver another grandson. My family lived then at 191 Hodge Avenue in Buffalo until 1941, when Mom and Dad were divorced. Ours was a comfortable, single-family house with a large backyard. A huge cherry tree graced the yard with a tall swing, and a playhouse with a wooden slide descending from its roof — ideal for winter sliding, and a great attraction for neighborhood kids.

Our maid, Juanita, was a plump, good-natured lady who lived on our third floor and knew how to be with young children. She often thought of interesting games and projects, such as helping us construct a simple, wooden bed tray in our basement colored in bright crayon drawings of palm trees and boats to surprise our mom during one of her illnesses. Juanita suggested to us boys the organizing of "The Cloud Club For Men Only," in a corner of our attic with a huge sign on the door. Her boyfriend, Kenny, would visit when Mother was away for the evening, and we wondered what transpired on the den couch when they thought we were asleep. There was no visual proof but many curious sounds.

On school days, Miss Johns, Grandfather Potter's office nurse, picked us up in her old Model T Ford sedan. The "hooga hooga" horn sounded in the driveway each morning as we donned mittens and scarfs. I graduated from the ninth grade at the School of Practice, part of the State Teachers College near the Albright Art Gallery, before our family moved to Greenfield, Massachusetts. Our school in Buffalo was a training ground for young teachers. More than 70 years later, I can clearly remember all my teachers' names — kindergarten through grade nine. Fifth grade veteran teacher, kindly Miss O'Reilly, made a life-long impression by asking me to stand red faced before the class and explain why I had taken a quarter from her desk to buy a slice of blueberry pie in the cafeteria because I was hungry.

I don't remember Dad ever living at home on Hodge Avenue. We never knew where he was, but realized that both our parents were unhappy, after 17 years of marriage, largely because of his alcoholism. As young children, we did not understand the situation, but seemed to take it for granted.

There were many good times in Buffalo, with almost daily visits to our Himmelsbach grandparents, nearby at 382 Elmwood Avenue. Grandfather George had his medical office at home, requiring absolute quiet much of the time. Jeanette and George Himmelsbach relished their grandchildren with a clever balance of authority and obvious love. The atmosphere and caring was ample proof of this, and I am sure carried over into our future lives. The high point and treat of any day was an invitation to stay for dinner. Nonna's outstanding meals, including homemade spiced pears, "fried mush" (sliced cold Cream of Wheat, fried in butter and swimming in "real" maple syrup). There were cookie jars and covered cake plates as well. Nothing could be better. I feel lucky to think of such long ago experiences.

L-R: Molly, Ben, and Grove

Benjamin Potter

Ben and Paul

Our Potter Grandparents:
Irving White Potter and Grace McDowell Potter
ଊଽ଼ଓ

Irving White Potter was my grandfather and an internationally known obstetrician who practiced for 56 years in Buffalo, New York. He was the son of Milton Grosvenor Potter, also a physician, who was professor of anatomy and dean of the University of Buffalo Medical School. Milton died of tuberculosis when he was 38. After his father's early death, Grandfather Irving was brought up in Syracuse, New York. He later returned to Buffalo to study medicine.

As there were no obstetrical specialists at the time, Irving began his practice as a family doctor, delivering many babies, usually at home. He told me that he worried at the number of babies who died in labor from lack of a timely delivery, presumably because caesarian section was major surgery then, and few doctors were trained to do this operation. Also, the complication rate was extremely high with surgical childbirth associated with the little known use of antibiotics and appropriate general anesthesia.

Grandfather Potter reintroduced and developed his own method of performing the internal podalic version procedure, which involved manually turning the baby from a head down to a feet-first or breech position for delivery. This was a controversial practice, and Irving spent a lifetime defending his method. Grandfather Potter reported in his book, *The Place of Version in Obstetrics* (Mosby Co., 1922), that his incidence of complications in new born deliveries using this method were the same or less than with the usual form of delivery. Grandfather Potter successfully delivered most of his patients, including his two children and the majority of Potter grandchildren. He became one of the early specialists in Obstetrics and Gynecology in the country, and a founding member of the American Colleges of Surgery and Ob-Gyn. During his 56-year practice, Irving Potter delivered 40,000 babies, a staggering figure by today's standards.

A workaholic, Grampa often nodded off in his big leather armchair in the living room to be ready for the next delivery at the Millard Fillmore Hospital. Irving charged his patients $50.00 for complete obstetrical care; and if they couldn't pay, the fee was forgiven. He had little idea of managing his money and was forced to declare bankruptcy during the Great Depression, losing his house and worldly assets. Our grandfather was extremely generous, paying tuition for 40 medical students at the University of Buffalo Medical School, and often not receiving repayment.

My two grandfathers, George Himmelsbach and Irving Potter, were classmates in medical school in Buffalo. They remained good friends their entire lives, despite the fact that their respective daughter and son, my parents, were divorced in 1941. Both men loved their grandchildren and were exemplary grandparents throughout both long lives.

Grandfather Irving was a spendthrift, while Dr. George was a superb businessman, who bought investment properties with carefully managed $3.00 office fees from his general practice — avoiding the stock market at all costs. The two men thrived on each other's company. On several occasions as a teenager, I drove them to Ob-Gyn meetings in Hot Springs, Virginia, while they visited in the back seat and occasionally complained about my fast driving. I usually hung a handkerchief over the speedometer to preserve the peace.

Irving Potter frequently entertained at luncheon in his Buffalo apartment, at 186 Chapin Parkway. Margaret, his housekeeper and cook, took such good care of my grandparents, whirring around the table set with white tablecloth and linen napkins, and serving full dinners each noon.

Grandmother Grace Potter, also in attendance at lunch, was so elderly and quiet that I remember very little about her. I do recall her being very kind, slowly swallowing a battery of pills at each meal. My dad, Milton Potter, Uncle Hugh McDowell, and cousin Robert McDowell, all practicing obstetricians, were frequent luncheon guests. The discussion was usually loud and medical in nature; and Grampa loved having his grandchildren at the table whenever possible. Perhaps this is where three grandsons, who all became obstetricians, got their start.

Grandfather Potter would frequently invite us to Newton's Restaurant, at the corner of Bryant Street and Delaware Avenue, after Sunday school. When his schedule allowed, we would attend the Shrine Circus, where he would roar with laughter at the clowns and seemed to enjoy the fun as much as we did.

Irving Potter was a gregarious, approachable man who laughed easily and relished chocolate candy and good food. He used to say that good food was not a waste of money. He neither smoked nor drank alcohol and seemed to require very little sleep. I remember the telephone ringing constantly with patients in labor, which explained the shortage of sleep time.

Benjamin Potter

He loved his practice and taught me the basics of dealing with patients. Grampa Potter believed that making one house call would insure seven new patients in the office. This is how I later increased my own practice in Concord, New Hampshire, when these visits were not the custom.

We were lucky to have the influence of such grandparents. Irving W. Potter died in 1956, at the age of 86. I always regretted not knowing grandmother Grace, who died many years before her husband

Irving and son Milton Potter at Hot Springs Medical Meeting.

Maternal Grandparents:
George Alexander Himmelsbach and Jeanette Potter Himmelsbach

My maternal grandfather, George A. Himmelsbach, MD, was born in 1867, in Buffalo, New York. He was the sixth of seven children. His parents, Joseph (1814-1881), and Catherine Bartholomew (1825-1913), Himmelsbach, were first-generation immigrants from the Baden Baden area of Germany, specifically, Bavaria Schultterthal. After their marriage, Joseph and Catherine lived at 35 Twelfth Street in Buffalo.

Grandfather George's siblings included Charles, who was blind and lived with his unmarried sister, Emma. Aunt Emma taught public school and coached me in arithmetic well into her 80s and 90s dying at 95 years. Phillip ran a grocery store at 370 Virginia Street in Buffalo, until his death at the age of 25. Julia married Fred Stewart, who ran a leather goods store in Buffalo.

When George's sister Ada was 23, she married William B. Knight. William and Ada subsequently divorced, and she married Harold Saxton. Ada and Harold lived in Mayville, New York. Their son, Harold Saxton, Jr., became a practicing physician in Mayville. Aunt Ada moved back to Buffalo in her later years. I can remember staying in her apartment on

Ashland Avenue when my mother was away. Ada had a bouncy step, and a twinkle in her eye, even as an elderly lady.

Grampa George also had a younger sister, Clarissa, who died at age two; and another sister, Sophia who I never knew and lived out of town, dying at age 74.

In 1891, at the age of 24, George Himmelsbach graduated from the Buffalo Medical College. Irving White Potter was George's classmate. Irving Potter's son, and my father, Milton G. Potter, Jr., would later marry George's oldest daughter, my mother, Helen Himmelsbach Potter.

Grandfather George married Jeanette Martha Potter shortly after she had graduated from the same Buffalo Medical School a year before George. She was one of seven daughters and eleven children of Roland Eaton Potter 1832-1921 and Mary Alice Shafer 1832-1905, and was born in Ithaca, New York on the family farm. Three of these young women became physicians, which was very unusual in the early twentieth century. Jeanette practiced medicine for a short while in Ithaca, but not after marriage in Buffalo, 1880. Grandmother Jeanette raised four daughters, Helen, Julia, Marion and Alice while overseeing her husband's practice. She was a loving and caring person, who provided abundant support to her husband and family. Jeanette hand stitched quilts on a huge, wooden frame in the upstairs "nursery" bedroom. She regularly produced crocks of delicious spiced pears, which were kept in the basement root cellar. The Himmelsbachs felt it was important to exchange work for meals with the homeless men who came to the kitchen door during the great depression, and I remember these people sitting on the back steps enjoying a hot, home cooked meal before starting work in the backyard.

Maternal Grandparents

George adored Jeanette until their dying days. He used to pat her cheek from behind her dining room chair after each meal. They were grandparents par excellence, and great role models for the younger generations. Jeanette could sew; and was a superb cook. When ever she disapproved of what we grandchildren were doing her favorite expression was "tut tut" with the waving of an index finger. I imagine Grandmother Himmelsbach had the patience of Job, for she stayed at home while George traveled alone to Europe every two years for a "rest." I never understood how that was arranged.

While Grampa George was private and quite stern, he was also very generous, and had a twinkle in his eye. He loved his grandchildren and welcomed us with endless invitations to dinner. We thought dinner at 382 Elmwood Avenue was much tastier than our meals at home. A favorite breakfast when we stayed overnight was "fried mush" which was sliced, fried Cream- of- Wheat, covered with butter and swimming in Vermont maple syrup. Grampa pretended to do the breast stroke from across the table when he saw how much syrup we poured on.

Grampa George ran his family practice from the house, so we grandchildren had to be very quiet during office hours. He had a bowl of smoking pipes on the mantelpiece in his cramped laboratory; and he used the Bunsen burner to light his pipes. I must have inherited his pipe smoking habit and his fondness for Edgeworth tobacco, for I used the same brand in my pipe for 60 years.

Grampa made house calls every afternoon, but on the odd afternoon, he would take his grandchildren across the Niagara River to Fort Erie in Canada on the ferryboat and return. He relished any boat life because he had crossed the Atlantic Ocean many times on his excursions to Europe. Another of our favorite jaunts was to the Lackawanna Railroad Station to watch the steam locomotives. Grampa George loved to take us on these trips for an hour or so between patient visits.

In addition to being an excellent physician and diagnostician, Grandfather George was a serious businessman. I suspect he knew where his first nickel was hidden. He charged patients $3.00 for each office visit, and was able to purchase a string of 20 rental properties around Buffalo. Real estate was Grampa George's investment of choice, not believing in the gamble of the stock market. This proved to be a magical stroke of luck during the Great Depression of the 1930s.

Grandparents Jeannette and George Himmelsbach

My Mother and Father:
Milton G. Potter and Helen Himmelsbach Potter
⊂ʒ⃟ଥ

My mother, Helen Himmelsbach Potter, was born in Buffalo, New York, in 1896. She was the oldest of four — Julia, Marion, and Alice were the younger sisters. All were born at home, at 382 Elmwood Avenue. Mother, or "Himmie," as her friends always called her, attended public school before leaving for four years at Smith College, (1918). Before it all ended, Grandfather Himmelsbach had produced four Smith College graduates, and quite possibly felt he owned the place.

Helen's life was an almost continuous social whirl. She was always very proud of this, and would boast about her many beaus, particularly during her college years. We heard many descriptions of the parties and dances she attended at Amherst and Williams colleges. We were told that Grandpa Himmelsbach had to step in more than once to get Mother into a more studious routine. This tale of social bliss continued into her 70s and 80s.

Our dad, Milton G. Potter, had been a social friend during the early Buffalo years, and during his time at Princeton. After World War I, my parents were married at a large wedding in Buffalo. Father began practicing obstetrics and gynecology with his father, Irving White Potter, MD.

My father had had a problem with alcohol before and during the Roaring Twenties. Over the course of 17 years, after Mother and Father were married, and when we four children were born, my dad's alcoholism became a serious family issue. We were told at an early age that our parents "toughed it out — for the sake of the children." In reality, divorces were not granted easily or quickly in New York State in the early 1940s.

In 1941, my parents finalized their divorce in Reno, Nevada. Only 16 years old, my brother Grove traveled west to act as legal witness to the proceedings. This was a difficult experience for Grove. In all my years growing up in Buffalo, I cannot remember my father and mother living together. When I realize the preciousness of a marriage, I shake my head. We survived to tell the tale.

Grandmother and Grandfather Himmelsbach stepped in and became almost surrogate parents during these years. We lived with Mother at numerous apartments and spent equal time at 382 Elmwood Ave., where we were always welcomed with open arms, despite my grandfather's busy medical practice in the same house.

Mother rented apartments at 47 Norwood Ave., 689 Linwood Ave., West Ferry St., and finally, Cleveland Ave., before she bought a small duplex on Arlington Park in the old section of Buffalo. Mother never worked outside the home. She must have possessed superhuman strength to shop for, feed, clothe, and raise four live-wire children. She was known to say many times: "You boys will be the death of me yet."

After WWII and the divorce, Mother often said that she would like to leave Buffalo and move "to a little white house in the country." In 1944, we moved to that little white house on Colerain Rd., in Greenfield, Massachusetts. This was five miles from town, and certainly in the country. With gas rationing still in effect, and a class "C" ration card — the lowest amount of gas allowed during the war — Mother fretted with boredom and loneliness in strange surroundings, and without her old Ford to zoom around in at leisure. My sister Molly was starting at Smith College, and Grove was still in the service. I worked at the Smeed Brother's dairy farm next door in Greenfield, and quite enjoyed myself.

Our saving grace was the three summer months on Cliff Island, Maine, which we all loved. The Cliff Island legacy began in 1939, when Tom Heath and his family — friends from Buffalo — suggested that "Himmie" bring the boys to the island. We first rented the Griffith house across from the island school, and then the Hodgekin Cottage at Oak Rock. The rent for the entire summer was $150.00. The Potters now own four houses on the island, the newest being my brother Paul's comfortable cape at Kennedy Beach. In 1956, Mother bought Guy Cobb's "Treetops," a three-room cottage near the dock for $2,700. She spent every summer there until she was in her mid-eighties. Lorene Potter and I now own this cottage together; and the Cliff Island legacy continues after seven decades.

Helen Potter was a strong personality. She never changed position on any issue. She loved and believed in her family above anything else. My mother was a fiercely independent lady who loved to travel wherever possible.

Mother knew all the antique dealers along Route 1 in New England. She was skillful at spotting and buying antique furniture at the lowest possible bid, and would rope priceless slant-top desks and tables to the car roof for transport from Maine to Buffalo. Smoking Carleton cigarettes was her great pleasure as she sped along.

Besides family, her life involved knitting, reading, and playing bridge. She was an excellent cook. She relished the Cliff Islanders, both summer and year-around folk, and once said that her greatest compliment was when elderly lobsterman, Charles Ricker, asked her to "go cook" with him in his house after his wife died.

In the late 1940s, we returned to Buffalo as home base, having spent time in Massachusetts and New Jersey. Mother purchased a small duplex on Arlington Park, which she maintained with income from the upstairs apartment. In 1948, I left for Phillips Academy in Andover, Massachusetts. Paul would follow me two years later. Grandfather Himmelsbach underwrote many expenses for my mother during these years.

Our mother was plagued with bi-polar syndrome. She experienced a debilitating depression every seven years. These episodes required hospitalization with electric shock therapy, medication, and psychotherapy. It was impossible to live with her during these sieges. However, on each occasion, after treatment and time, life would begin again for her. In her early 90s, our mother moved from one assisted living home to another. My youngest brother, Paul, orchestrated all this. He took Himmie out for Friday night dinner every week. Paul began with a martini, and Mother with her V-8 juice. Despite suffering from severe dementia, it was our mother's greatest joy to look forward to Paul's dinner dates.

One week before my mother's death at age 94, my wife Judy encouraged me to make a round trip visit from New Hampshire to Buffalo, for a final good bye. Mother was uncommunicative. After helping with her lunch, I arrived home to New Hampshire in time for dinner. It was a good

Mother and Father

day. This was the end of an era.

My dad, Milton G. Potter, was born in Buffalo, in 1897, into the family of a very busy practicing OB-GYN, Irving White Potter. Father attended public school until high school, when he enrolled at the Nichols School. He became a well-rounded athlete at Nichols, playing football, among other sports. Pictures of him at the time show a handsome boy. Apparently my dad was popular socially, which continued through the travels of life.

Milt entered Princeton in the class of 1919, where, in his own words, he "had difficulty scholastically." He entered Cottage Club, along with F. Scott Fitzgerald. Apparently, Scott and Zelda "carried on" every weekend, as did the rest of the members. Dad told me that late at night, he helped Scott Fitzgerald proofread excerpts from *This Side of Paradise*.

It was a time of black waiters who came to the table to take meal orders: "How would you like your eggs, sir?"

This was a far cry from what future generations would experience, even at Princeton. My brothers Grove and Paul, and my daughter, Heather all attended Princeton.

Partway through his Princeton years, during World War I, my father left college to join the Buffalo General Hospital Ambulance Corps in France. His father arranged for Milt to be outfitted with a Brooks Brothers sleeping bag for cold nights. Dad seldom spoke of the experience. It was a hard time, one that is difficult to contemplate. Likewise, my brother Paul would seldom speak of his experiences during the Vietnam War.

After the army years, our father returned to Princeton where he did "Phi Beta Kappa-quality work," as compared to the pre-war days. Upon graduation, Milt entered the University of Buffalo Medical School, from where his father and grandfather had graduated. Dad was a very bright person, and a superb physician and surgeon. He started work with his father after graduation in a very busy obstetrics and gynecology practice, during a time when Irving Potter had become nationally known for his promotion and wide use of the internal podalic version method of delivery.

Grandfather Potter was often invited to lecture around the world on his delivery technique. Because Grandfather was prone to seasickness, and there were few airplanes at the time, he would send Dad to read the scientific papers and defend the obstetrical delivery method, which was new and controversial. Milt enjoyed these trips. He told me that he usually sent the professor's wife a dozen roses before the meeting. This was so typical of my father. He knew his way around the circuit.

From early in life, it was apparent to me that Dad had an alcohol problem. During his later years, he was on and off the wagon many times. Grandfather Potter would cover Dad's patients for him during the drinking periods. Dad became a friend of William (Bill) Wilson, the founder of Alcoholics Anonymous. I wrote my senior thesis at Dartmouth College on AA; and my father arranged a luncheon for me to meet Mr. Wilson at Jack Dempsey's restaurant in New York City. This man was a tower of friendliness and information; and that meeting deeply influenced my thinking and me.

During my senior year at Dartmouth, my father went beyond expectation to contact his colleagues regarding my entrance to medical school. His efforts were endless even though my grades were less than outstanding. I was accepted at McGill Medical School in Montreal; and it was the best of all schools for me. I was pleased and felt very lucky to be in graduate school. While I was studying in the city, Dad was invited to give a paper at the Montreal Obstetrical Society. I attended the dinner meeting at the Ritz-Carlton Hotel, sat at the head table with him, and was very proud. He was an excellent public speaker. He often told me that when speaking before a group, it was best to speak directly to a person in the back row, so everyone could hear. This thought proved useful to me as I began to speak publicly myself.

During the summer following my third year of medical school, I was an extern at King Edward VII Hospital in Bermuda. These were such important months for I met, and later married, a beautiful nurse, Johanna Broughall from Toronto. We were married in 1957, in June, and my father was best man in our wedding. This meant a lot to him, as he was a great admirer of my new bride, and the Canadian Broughall family.

My mother and father were mismatched in many ways. Dad did not seem to understand the meaning of family — though I am sure he loved and was proud of his children. During our young years – before and after the divorce – Dad would simply disappear for long periods. I am sure that his alcoholism was a significant factor. He once told me that the divorce never should have occurred. My mother had different ideas.

Milt's three boys, Grove, Paul and Ben, all OB-GYNs, gathered in Buffalo to celebrate his 70th birthday. To mark the occasion, we performed a vaginal hysterectomy at Millard Fillmore Hospital. The anesthesiologist snapped a memorable picture from the head of the operating table. We gathered afterward for a happy luncheon.

In his later life, Milton Potter's major goal became attending his 50th Princeton reunion. He did so in full form. While we were growing up, every five years our family would travel to

Princeton for the reunion. We always marched with the class of 1919 in the parade. After the reunion, we would drive down to the Jersey shore for a deep-sea fishing trip with Dad. These are all happy memories.

I concluded that Dad did not understand growing children, or how to deal with them. The opposite was true in later life when we could talk "medical shop," and became good friends. In Buffalo, my brothers Grove and Paul stood by Dad until the end. They continued his practice, eventually taking it over completely, as he had done from his father.

Deep depression set in during his 73rd year; and Dad stopped eating. This ended his life at home in Eggertsville, New York. Paul had moved in to care for him. I felt badly that I could not have been there to help. My father was a talented man in so many ways, but less so in others. Dad was a spendthrift like his father. Both were great men who lacked business sense; and Dad died without savings. However, his life ended with the satisfaction of knowing that his three sons were carrying on the family medical tradition; and his daughter once worked as the assistant to the dean of Dartmouth Medical School. I wish that he had lived a longer life.

My father and mother dealt with great depression over the course of their lives. Both were good people who loved their families, and encouraged us along our paths so well.

Mother and Father

Mother at Smith College

My father and I

1st Annual Irving Potter Memorial Lecture by Greenhill, June 1959 – L-R: Paul, Grove, Dad, and Ben

Four Children: Grovesnor, Molly Scheu, Paul, and Ben

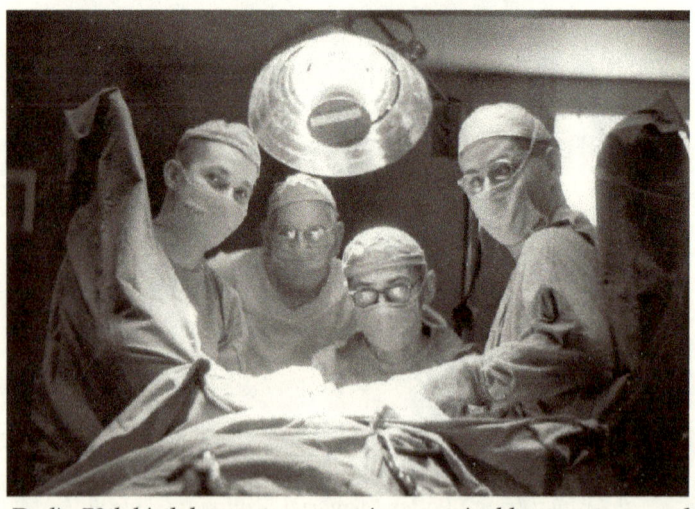

Dad's 70th birthday party, overseeing a vaginal hysterectomy and repair. L-R: Grove, Dad, Paul, and Ben

Helen Potter: 80th Birthday at Cliff Island

"Treetops": Our Cliff Island house in winter

Great Aunt Molly: Mary Grosvenor Potter
ಛಿಜಿ

Mary Grosvenor Potter, Great Aunt Molly, was Irving White Potter's only sibling. The family lived in Buffalo until their father, and Dean of the University of Buffalo Medical School, Milton Grosvenor Potter, died of tuberculosis at age 38. Their mother, Clara Chase Potter (1842-1896), was left to raise both children – first in Syracuse with friends, and then in Buffalo.

In 1898, at the age of 27, Aunt Molly would ride the train to New York City from Buffalo. She clerked in a law office while studying the law, passing her bar exam in New York. Aunt Mollie became one of the first women lawyers in the state, unusual in those days. She opened her own law office, began practice, living on East 30th Street. Her first office boy was Fiorello LaGuardia, who she described as a bright little Italian boy who later became the colorful Mayor of New York City. He often wore a dirty shirt to work in her office. Aunt Molly quickly remedied this situation by sending him to Macy's Department Store for a new one.

Molly later moved to 239 ½ East 48th Street, an old brownstone, which later became our home headquarters whenever we were in New York City. Her apartment had previously served as headquarters for our dad when he was a student at Princeton (1919), and afterwards.

The brownstone on East 48th Street backed onto the Turtle Bay Gardens. Each house had a small garden with a wrought iron fence and statuary. It was quite a contrast to the busy street in front of the house. Kathryn Hepburn lived across the garden and occasionally gave Aunt Molly opening night tickets to a Broadway play, which we nephews could sometimes use.

Aunt Molly's maid, Nettie, came from a slave family in Alabama. She lived with Aunt Molly for over 50 years as cook and housekeeper. She was a superb cook, as we knew from many, many meals while visiting. Nettie never left the house. She did not believe in banks, and hid all of her cash earnings in shoeboxes under her bed.

As a successful practicing attorney, Aunt Molly was able to maintain a motorboat at the 79th Street Marina. Instead of doing business at a country club or restaurant, Molly would take her clients out for a spin on the Hudson River. Aunt Molly relied on a Puerto Rican captain, to maintain and drive the boat.

Aunt Molly was indomitable. When my mother and father were married in the late 1920s, Aunt Molly traveled up the Hudson River and across the Erie Canal to Buffalo, a journey which took two weeks. The captain got drunk one night and burned up the boat, ending our aunt's seafaring days.

Aunt Molly was truly Avant-garde. She always had the latest of gadgets from Macy's Department Store; and she encouraged us to use her pale green Dodge whenever we needed it. She owned one half of the Charlesgate Hotel, on the Fenway in Boston, with Mrs. Summers. From time to time, we stayed at the Charlesgate with Aunt Molly, and attended a Red Sox game at nearby Fenway Park. Molly was a devoted Ted Williams fan.

Our great aunt had type 2 diabetes, and never missed her six-month check-ups with Dr. Elliot Joslin, founder of the Joslin Clinic. Mollie was one of his first diabetic patients. The old doctor was still at the Clinic when I was a resident at the Boston Lying In Hospital many years later (1959-1962). I can clearly remember Dr. Joslin parading around the outpatient clinic in a three-piece tweed suit.

In her later years Aunt Mollie lived with her niece, Virginia Anderson, my dad's only sister, on Colonial Circle in Buffalo. Mollie never married but succeeded in loving all of her nieces and nephews. We loved her too. She was kind beyond a doubt, good and generous to us all. She died of natural causes at 92.

Grandfather Potter, Aunt Molly

Moving About: The School Years, 1945-1949

In 1945, when I was 15 and Paul was 13, we moved with Mother to 22 Plymouth Street, in Montclair, New Jersey. We moved from Greenfield, Massachusetts, at the invitation of Aunt Alice and Uncle Hobey Agnew. Alice Agnew was my mom's youngest sister. Hobey was a busy ophthalmologist in Montclair who enabled us to live in his recently renovated second floor apartment above the office. It seemed very fancy with red kitchen counter tops.

Paul and I knew practically no one in Montclair, and were enrolled in the Hillside Middle School. I soon knew Craig Hibben, a neighbor and school mate from nearby Clinton Ave., as well as Townsend Albright. None of us were particularly athletic, so we hung out together after school. My grades were unimpressive; but my homeroom and science teacher, Richard Tewksbury, instilled an interest in science and non-team, outdoor sports. He had trekked from California to South America along the Pan-American Highway during summer vacations and sprinkled salty stories from his travels into his classes.

During our years in New Jersey, I spent frequent weekends with Uncle Hobey at his Whipperwill Springs Farm, on

Greenwood Lake, in northern New Jersey. I was learning to ride Old Red, an unexcitable and friendly horse, and generally enjoyed the farm and outdoor work. Uncle Hobey acted as a surrogate father during those years and was very kind to us all. Along with a few other choice habits, Hobey taught us to pee off the back porch steps after dark. We were always grateful for the Agnew's generosity during those early teenage years. After retirement and a move to Dorset, Vermont, Uncle Hobey suffered greatly and died from a painful prostate cancer.

I attended Montclair High School through junior year, when I tried out for the varsity baseball team. Clary Anderson, the coach, threw me three pitches, all of which I missed, and said, "That's all, Potter. Come back next year." So much for the baseball team!

At that stage in our lives, Aunt Julia and Uncle Sherman Holcomb, another of Mother's four sisters and my godparents, who lived in Beverly Farms, Massachusetts, decided that I, and later Paul, should enter Phillips Andover Academy. Uncle Sherman had attended Andover many years ago before studying at Yale. I applied and received a 50% scholarship. I started in the fall of 1947 as an upper middler, a repeat junior, third year for me after finishing my junior year at Montclair High School. I graduated with the Class of 1949.

Those years at Andover were two semi-satisfying years in my life. I worked hard, thinking each week that I would flunk out. It was far more difficult than public high school. Andre Machain was my roommate in Adams Hall and a serious student. We met again years later when living near each other in New Hampshire during our professional years. Andy was a CPA in nearby Contoocook.

Moving About

The first year at Andover was not a happy one, but it did end successfully. I moved on to my senior year as proctor for 50 freshman students in Williams Hall. Mary and Douglas Dunbar were housemasters who were a wonderful couple who knew the preparatory school life well. My proctor partners were Win Jordan from Worcester, MA., Clem Hastie from the Boston area, and Barry Phelps from Rochester, N.Y. These three classmates became lifelong friends; and my experiences with them had a lasting effect. Barry was an usher in my Toronto wedding to Joey Broughall. I roomed with Win Jordan in Williams Hall. We were responsible for 50 lively kids in the dining room and during the evening homework hours. I received a stipend of $900.00, half the Andover tuition. This job appeared to save the day for me at Andover.

Before I graduated, Dean Benedict asked me where I wanted to go to college. When I said, "Dartmouth College," he advised me not to apply anywhere else. He picked up the phone and called the Admissions Department at Dartmouth. That was the end of it.

My father quickly said, "Don't pay any attention to that fellow at Andover, and to apply to all 10 or 12 other colleges just in case."

I graduated from Dartmouth in the class of 1953. College admissions are far more difficult now than ever before; and consequently I worry about my nine grandchildren and all others in their efforts toward a top education. Dartmouth President John Sloan Dickey impressed on us that a liberal arts education sets the stage for a balanced life, regardless of profession or vocation. I have found this to be absolutely true.

Benjamin Potter

Roommates at Andover, Class of 1949
L-R: Ben Potter, Barry Phelps, Clem Hastie

At Sea for Two Summers
1951-1952
⊂₈₨⊃

In 1951, as a sophomore at Dartmouth College, I signed aboard the Blue Dolphin, a 100-foot Bluenose schooner, built in Shelburne, Nova Scotia. I would spend the summer as dishwasher and cabin boy on a subarctic research expedition to the coast of Labrador.

Skipper David "Beany" Nutt, in his late 30s, had been the youngest full commander in the U.S. Navy during WWII. After the war, he had purchased the schooner, which had been on antisubmarine patrol, in the North Atlantic, and was previously the private yacht of the Pepperrells of Saco, Maine. The crew of 19 was made up of researchers of all stripes: oceanographers from Woods Hole; foresters; a Dartmouth medical student, who did chemical studies of ocean water and currents; and radio operator, engineer, and first mate Reggie Wilcox. Wilcox was from Newfoundland and had been with Captain Bob Bartlett on countless expeditions to the Arctic. The Norwegian boatswain was also a colorful character. Many of these men were professional schooner sailors.

We sailed from Boothbay Harbor in early June, accompanied out of harbor by Admiral MacMillan and his schooner Bowdoin, which was also headed to the Arctic Ocean for a summer expedition. We sailed from Boothbay to the Straights of Belle Isle, off the northern tip of Newfoundland, on one tack lasting four days and 22 hours — a huge jump with steady southwest winds.

We approached Lake Melville, a long estuary into the southern Labrador coast to Northwest River, one of the Grenfell Association's medical outposts. There we met Dr. Anthony Paddon, the Labrador doctor who visited all the coastal communities by dogsled in the winter, and on the hospital ship, Maravel, during ice-free summer months. We ran into him frequently in our travels. He would always fire a cannon salute across our bow, then come aboard dressed in a blue blazer and tie, for a cup of coffee and pie before proceeding on his rounds. We took aboard in Northwest River a trapper, Harvey Montague, who served as the shore guide for our forester, who did tree surveys along the coast. Harvey entertained at his house every summer with homebrew that he had "put down" the year before. The brew must have been 100 proof or better. Those were parties never to be forgotten. Twenty-five years later when my daughter Heather, at age 15, served as a housemother at the orphanage in Northwest River, she met Harvey Montague, who regaled her with Blue Dolphin stories from years before. Heather said "Dad, I couldn't believe all the stories that Harvey told me about you and your group." So it goes.

The following summer of 1952, my brother Paul and I traveled to Boothbay Harbor for the farewell party before the Blue Dolphin sailed off on its next expedition, but I had not planned to go on this trip. During the evening, Reggie Wilcox told me that the professional cook had not turned up for the sailing, having been up in the Village Inn with his girlfriend. Wilcox said the skipper wanted me to go as cook until another replacement could be found at the Hudson's Bay Company in Goose Bay, Labrador.

I agreed to go along if Paul could go as the dishwasher. This was agreed upon. We had no clothes, and would leave our mother's car on the dock for her to retrieve. The cook had previously stored $10,000 of groceries in the galley, and I knew where nothing was — nary a cookbook either. We shoved off with the Bowdoin again, and the usual flotilla leading out of harbor — horns blowing and very festive. On the way across the Gulf of Maine, we called Mother at Cliff Island on the ship-to-shore radio to say that we would return in three months and that her car was on the dock in Boothbay. She was speechless.

Thus started a great experience for both of us. We used the emergency clothing held for anyone rescued along the way, and took a survey of all the 19 crew members gleaning all each of them knew about cooking. I kept all these sheets of paper as my primary cookbook, and pawed through the mounds of food stowed aboard. It was a slow start, but a good one. There was never one complaint heard from anyone concerning my cooking or the food, but it was the hardest work that I had ever done. Bread baking started with twelve lead-like loaves on the first few tries, but then took on a more normal look and taste. These guys ate 24-hours-a-day, so hearty fare had to be ready at all times.

Paul and I slept in the forecastle beside the galley, on pipe berths. We had our own toilet in the forepeak, with a slatted, bar-like swinging door. With only one other head on board, the men frequently charged into our territory. Problem solved by nailing down a pair of boots to the cabin sole, making it look as though someone was already sitting down. This trick worked only for a while.

We sailed non-stop to Labrador, and once into the Straights

of Belle Isle —north of Newfoundland — we encountered many sized icebergs which, had broken off the Greenland ice fields and floated south in the Davis Straight to meet us. These were pre-radar days; so that the schooner navigated through the ice fields with the lookout— in the crow's nest barrel on the foremast - shouting by megaphone to the helmsman to steer our way through the small growlers, ice bits, and the larger icebergs. There were no radios or radar at the time to communicate our directions, or to enable our schooner to navigate at night, or through fog, along the rocky coast. It was exciting work; and we all took our turns in the barrel to protect any contact with our wooden hull.

There were enough stories to tell - and vivid memories from these two voyages - to last a lifetime.

A Broadband Trip through Europe
1954
○3⁊○

Following my second year at McGill Medical School, I imagined the idea of an extended trip to Europe, largely financed by money I had earned catching and selling lobsters as a young boy on Cliff Island, ME, with my brother, Paul. The other stimulus was my California cousin, Ben Nyce's offer to sell me an old Austin A-40 for $800. Ben had crashed into a cow the previous summer, and had the car stored in Paris. To swing this deal, I needed three partners. I recruited Ross McIntyre, a pre-med classmate at Dartmouth; Arthur Dawson, a McGill medical student; and Drew McTaggert, also a medical student in Montreal, and himself a mountain climber from British Columbia.

McTaggert would only accept our offer if we agreed to spend a week in Zermatt, Switzerland, to acclimate and climb the Matterhorn. I had never climbed more than the hills around Hanover, New Hampshire, but this didn't seem to be a problem. We were off.

I crossed the Atlantic on an ocean liner — leaving Quebec City and landing in Southampton. It was an ancient Holland American, globe circling cruise ship; and it seemed unusually plush. I traveled with Dawson, who wangled his way up to first class, while I was below the waterline in steerage. It was exciting and fun taking seven days to reach England. I traveled to Devonshire to visit family friends before meeting Ross McIntyre in Trafalgar Square. The three of us crossed the English Channel from Dover to Dieppe, then continued on to Paris, where we met McTaggert and the old car — less damaged than we had thought.

After driving to Germany and Heidelberg, then on to Munich and Cologne, we arrived in Vienna, where my dad, Milton G. Potter, was presenting a paper at a medical meeting. We motored into the city behind the cavalcade of then U.S. Secretary of State John Foster Dulles — a good means to enter a strange city. Mr. Dulles was attending a meeting with the Russians and British. The three allies then controlled Austria after World War II. We ventured out of our boarding house that night to have a tasty dinner at the hotel with my father.

We inched down to Zermatt from Vienna, through the Italian Alps, arriving in a farmer's hayloft. For one Swiss franc a night, we slept for a week on our mound of hay, gazing at the majestic, 14,500 foot Matterhorn when the clouds opened and allowed. Our routine was to train on local mountain trails in rented climbing boots until noon, then to enjoy the town of Zermatt itself. There were no cars in Zermatt and, by chance, the Swiss national holiday, August 4, was celebrated that week. It was an unusual and happy way to "train" for my first mountain ascent.

After convincing two Swiss brothers — both professional mountain guides — to lead our expedition, we roped as we climbed, and arrived at the 10,000 foot Hernley Hut on the first night of the ascent. After supper and a brief sleep, the guides woke us at 3:00 a.m., to begin the climb to the summit

A Broadband Trip through Europe

at 14,500 feet. Poor Arthur Dawson's legs became frozen with terror, so we bedded him down in a Red Cross hut with chocolates and oranges, and started our climb. I had never climbed a major mountain before, especially with ropes and pitons, so the exercise was pretty daunting. It was fine if one didn't look downhill. We reached the summit at 9:00 a.m. There was a helping rope cabled to the mountain for the last 50 yards, but I was exhausted. I recovered partially after a swallow of brandy from a kind French climber. The summit view was obliterated by a blinding summer snowstorm.

The descent of the Matterhorn was another story — much more difficult than the ascent. Our guides rappelled us down on climbing ropes around our waists, using pitons fastened into the mountainside. I kept noticing a small white church through my legs below us in Zermatt. We were to jump from one outcropping to the next, straight out from the mountain — hardly a natural move.

The three of us arrived in the valley without mishap. I was so exhausted I slept for 24 hours straight. Arthur Dawson, who we had abandoned below, was hale and hearty after his sleep in the hut.

It was foolish of me to climb the Matterhorn without training. However, at 24 years of age, who would not accept a challenge like this? Later in life, I have noticed a new, almost panic-like fear of heights, but interestingly, not of airplanes.

This trip influenced my life in many colorful new experiences and marvelous memories, which include Venice, Rome, and the Pyrenees. The Four Musketeers returned to Paris, sold the car, and embarked from Rotterdam to end the grand circle in Quebec City – in time to begin the next year of medical school in Montreal.

After climbing the Matterhorn
L-R: Dawson, Potter, Guide, McTaggert, McIntyre, Guide

Johanna Broughall Potter:
October 29, 1932-December 16, 1994
෴

As a third year student at the McGill Medical School in Montreal, I was very lucky to obtain an externship at the King Edward VII Hospital in Hamilton, Bermuda. It was there I spent the summer of 1956.

This was the start of a life-changing experience for me, both personally and professionally. I was on this island as a student — assisting at surgery, suturing motorbike lacerations in the Emergency Room, learning to deliver babies, and attending medical rounds with the staff physicians. It was the chance of a lifetime.

One morning, while making patient rounds with Doctor Lang, he described a patient with a serious sun blister infection of the upper lip. The patient didn't want visitors to call because of the nasty looking infection. After one look at this beautiful patient, my future was sealed. Joey, a graduate nurse from Sick Children's Hospital in Toronto, was in Bermuda for one year of nursing experience. Little did she know...

We were married two days after my medical school graduation the following year — May 25, 1957 — at Saint Paul's Anglican Church in Toronto.

Our first child, Heather, was born during the medical

residency years in Boston, followed by Ben in 1962, and finally by John in 1967. Both boys were born after settling in Concord, New Hampshire at 9 Pine Street. Our kids were born healthy, and fortunately have remained healthy all of their lives. Joey was a caring pediatric nurse, and a very wise mother, who was left with most of our children's care because I was constantly away from home, trying to start an obstetric and gynecologic practice at the Concord Clinic. Joey had impeccable judgment in most family situations, and was able to be home with the children during those early years.

Having moved from the duplex at Pine Street to our final home at 31 Westbourne Road in 1966, Joey began to have vague symptoms of blurring vision and arm pain. She was in her early forties. A final diagnosis of Multiple Sclerosis was not made for two years. Gradually these symptoms increased, requiring a wheelchair and almost continual nursing care during the day. Joey never gave in to her physical problems. This was true throughout 24 years of illness. When finally becoming immobile at home, she wondered, "What will I do now?"

Though having never written formally, Joey decided to become an author and record her observations and reactions to her illness and the world around her. Though finally unable to manually write or type, she dictated three volumes of short essays to her many visitors. *A Different Point of View*, *Thoughts by Joey*, and *Joey's Work*, written over a ten-year period, were privately published by Peter Randall of Portsmouth, New Hampshire. These books were well received and sold in bookstores around the state. Joey had found her positive niche and project, which gave great personal strength to her — and later to a growing group of readers and supporters. She needed to be involved in helping others as she had always done as a nurse. These little books taught so many of us the importance of simplicity, human nature, and the beauty of everyday life.

My sister, Molly Scheu, and her husband Ed, arranged for us to own a hydraulic lift wheelchair van in fine condition. This enabled me to bring Joey home several times weekly for dinner throughout the nine years she lived at the nursing home. This was an emotional lifesaver for us both, as it kept her, at least partially, in touch with her home surroundings. We often ended the return dinner expedition after the facility doors were locked, irritating the nurses noticeably. Over 1,400 round trips to our home in Concord made it all worthwhile.

On December 16, 1994, Joey died peacefully at Pleasant View Health Care, where she had lived for nine years. This was the site of Mary Baker Eddy's summer home in Concord. Our three children, Heather, Ben, and John Paul, wrote material at the Concord Library for her Memorial Service, the day before it occurred at Saint Paul's Church, before a standing-room-only crowd. David Jones, our minister, presented Hannah Rose Potter, our recently born first grandchild, who Joey had seen briefly before her death, to the congregation saying, "I present to you the new Joey Potter."

The Joey Potter Memorial Loan Fund, made possible by the generosity of family and friends, was raised for our church. The New Hampshire Community Loan Fund invested and managed Joey's fund, which was to be loaned — at low interest rates — to those wishing to start small businesses or buy first homes. The fund will last in perpetuity in her name, and is owned by the church in Joey's memory.

This was the end of a loving and important life: wife, mother and great friend. She, with a quick and dry sense of Canadian humor. We had learned to have our "window on the world."

Johanna Broughall Potter

Ben and Joey at Mt. Rainer

Joey on Monhegan Island, Maine

Benjamin Potter

Joey and young Ben out for a spin

L-R: Heather, Emma Maynard, and Mary Moon at John's Wedding, Vermont

Johanna Broughall Potter

John (20), Ben (25), Heather (28), and Ulysses (3)

Rotating Internship, Charity Hospital, New Orleans, Louisana: (1957-1958)

After our wedding in Toronto, on May 25, 1957, and a honeymoon on Martha's Vineyard, Joey and I set out for my internship year at Charity Hospital in New Orleans. Much to Joey's dismay, we traveled in a second-hand, blue Plymouth sedan purchased with wedding gift money. All our worldly possessions were packed tightly aboard, with a flowerpot on top of the pile.

Once in New Orleans, we holed up in a motel with a bottle of Bourbon and the *Times Picayune* newspaper to look for digs. We came upon a duplex apartment in Metairie, a suburb of New Orleans, for $90.00 per month. Lo and behold, we soon found that the young lady in the other apartment was a high-priced prostitute, with a clientele of upper level state government executives from Baton Rouge, the state capitol. Our neighbor was a former Bourbon Street dancer who was being "protected" by a Louisiana state trooper. No other neighbor in Metairie ever became friendly – knowing that I was a young doctor, the neighbors assumed we were in charge of health problems in our building.

Joey immediately got a job in the surgical recovery room at Charity Hospital; and I started my rotating intern year with a month on the midnight shift, riding a bright red Cadillac ambulance to all parts of New Orleans and southern Louisiana, knowing little of what I was doing. We were on opposite schedules, so we would meet in the parking lot to exchange our only car and a kiss good night. Such a way to begin a new marriage.

It was a year to remember — working in a hospital with 3,000 beds, 98% black patients, and 12,000 births a year. I was to spend one or two months in each of the major specialties, and I will never forget it. The hospital was one of a chain set up by King Fish Governor, Huey Long, to provide free medical care for the poor of Louisiana. I earned $75.00 per month during that year. Joey earned $250.00 as a graduate nurse, so dollars were scarce and we spent them wisely.

At the time, my sister, Molly Scheu, lived in Mobile, Alabama. For Christmas, she gave us a nine-inch GE television, which buoyed our spirits considerably. Our hobby while in New Orleans was to visit as many antebellum plantations in Mississippi and Louisiana as possible. The heat and humidity were unbearable and enough to make plans to come north for residency training in Boston.

We celebrated year's end with dinner at Antoine's Restaurant on Bourbon Street in the French Quarter. The bill was two months of my wages; and I had to be cleared for honesty with a call by the maître d' to my hospital administrator to arrange for later payment.

While in New Orleans, Joey had an early miscarriage. She was operated on late at night at Charity Hospital by Dr. Milton McCall, a world renowned Gynecologic surgeon, and my department chief in Obstetrics who was also our neighbor in Metairie, and came for a house call while I was on duty at the hospital. So many experiences to remember vividly.

In June of 1958, Joey and I made our way to Boston to begin my four-year residency in Ob-Gyn and General Surgery. I said "three cheers" for the cooler, less humid weather. We traveled north to Boston in the old car, having learned and seen so much of the south in a short year, including a sound medical experience.

Deep South to True North
1958-1962
ଔଃ୫ଠ

Driving north to New England, away from 93 degree midnight temperatures, Joey and I were gloating and cooling. Arriving in Boston to start four years of residency training, we moved in with Aunt Julia and Uncle Sherman Holcomb for three weeks. My godparents were kind enough to let us bunk in while we looked for an apartment.

I started a one-year rotation in General Surgery at Malden Hospital. I was waiting for the next opening rotation in Ob-Gyn at Harvard Medical School. We settled at 14 Lilly Street in Malden, and stayed there for four years. Soon little Heather arrived and was the hit of the party. Joey worked as a pediatric nurse at Malden Hospital until Heather arrived, and then became a stay-at-home mother. After the surgical rotation with Tom Griffiths and Malcolm Brochin in Malden, I began commuting to the Longwood Avenue Lying-In Hospital (now Brigham and Women's Hospital) in Boston, where I worked as a lowly house officer.

I found that a few senior staff members at the Boston Lying-In Hospital were completely self-oriented. These were nationally known doctors who were excellent teachers, but were involved with busy practices and their Harvard appointments. Others were devoted to teaching their resident doctors. Doctors Arthur Tucker and Luke Gillespie were willing to help and teach us day or night.

Our professor and Department Chairman, Dr. Duncan Reid, had no significant connection with some of his residents. To me, he seemed distant and disconnected on first meeting. Having come from a large public hospital where the interns delivered every pregnant patient who came through the door, I delivered a set of twins in the middle of the night at the Lying-In, and then went back to sleep. The next morning, I was called to Dr. Reid's office. He criticized me for not calling a more senior doctor for the twin delivery, and said that he had already called my father about the matter.

I said, "What did the old man say?"

"Why don't you fire him?" Dad had asked.

Dr. Reid replied that I had only been there a week, so he couldn't fire me. That was my entry into Boston medicine.

My residency years involved 18 months in Obstetrics at the Boston Lying-In Hospital, and 18 months in Gynecology at the Free Hospital for Women in Brookline. I was much happier at the latter, with a great Chief, Dr. George Van S. Smith, who understood people — and his resident doctors — well. He was made of whole cloth. He trusted us, and we him. I think that gynecology became my favorite part of practice, perhaps because of Dr. Smith.

Long after he retired from the medical faculty, I visited Dr. Smith at his home on Upland Road in Brookline. His wife, Olive, a well-known endocrine researcher had died first, leaving Dr. Smith with his unedited, but completed memoirs. He asked me to edit and review his entire life story, which came as a real surprise. Dr. Smith died before I had finished the job; but I sent my original copy to his son, Gardner, who was a professor of surgery at Johns Hopkins and a classmate of mine at Andover (1949). Before going to Harvard Medical School, George Smith had also graduated from Andover. He was my favorite person of all the residency years.

Dr. Smith always asked about my family and children by name, and truly cared. Interestingly, his son Gardner told me at an Andover reunion that his dad was never home, and paid little attention to his children as they grew up. This seems true of many great men — they become so embroiled in their career or profession, there is no time for anything else.

On balance, I felt that I received a lot of education during my Harvard residency, but not as much practical experience as I might have had. In contrast, my brothers Grove and Paul both trained in Obstetrics and Gynecology at Bellevue Hospital in New York City, which was similar to Charity Hospital where I had interned. There was little formal education at Bellevue, but Grove and Paul learned by experience, with senior teaching staff around much of the time. These were different teaching philosophies. My training prepared me well for the practice years; and looking back I am very grateful for my time in Boston. Joey and I scrimped through this time on very little money. In the end, it all was worthwhile.

Wending towards Concord, New Hampshire: 1962

ೞೲ

In 1962, upon finishing my medical residency in Boston, I passed up a practice position in Beverly, Massachusetts, in favor of one at the Concord Clinic in Concord, New Hampshire. This turned out, many years later, to be the correct choice. I began my medical work there. Joey and I felt that we had made the right choice and settled in.

We rented a duplex apartment at 9 Pine Street, in downtown Concord, one week before Benjamin Broughall Potter, our second child, was born at the Boston Lying-In Hospital on May 3, 1962. The house was an old Victorian with a furnace that struggled mightily to heat the place well. Our rent was $90.00 per month. We froze to death for four winters, but lived happily with two young children and a beginning practice in Obstetrics and Gynecology at the old Concord Clinic at 19 Pillsbury Street.

I became the partner of Dr. Thomas Ritzman, one of the two obstetricians in Concord. Also in our multispecialty group were Drs. Homer Lawrence, Maurice Green, Warren Eberhart, William Penhale, Bud Gouchoe, Munro Proctor, Joe Ward, and Chuck Murray. I began practice in a comfortable office in the private wing of the old Margaret Pillsbury Hospital at a starting annual salary of $10,000. I felt like a millionaire.   Joey and I were thrilled to be on our way, after the endless training and five years of marriage. We stayed in our apartment for four years before purchasing our dream house at 31 Westbourne Road from Frank and Loretta Kenison in 1966. This proved to be a wonderful family headquarters until I retired and it was sold in 1997. Having lived in a succession of apartments growing up in Buffalo, New York, this home on Thayers Pond was where we hoped to stay. We did for 31 years. I also found that everyone at the Concord Clinic and Concord Hospital was welcoming and friendly, so we were off to a flying start and many great experiences.

Joey had been a pediatric nurse all of her professional life, and took a job with the Visiting Nurse Association before John Paul Potter was born, and our family completed. In Joey's fortieth year, double vision and arm weakness crept in. We made many visits to Dr. Ralph Hunter, neurologist at Dartmouth Medical School; but no firm diagnosis was made for two years. Eventually, multiple sclerosis was found, and the long, 24-year progression began.

Joey refused to cave in under any circumstances, and continued to manage our children's school, sports, and home lives, in my perpetual absence. Joey had the knack for nearly perfect judgment in most situations. She knew when to stop driving her spiffy blue car, for fear of injuring someone, when she was no longer able to reach the brake pedal at a busy intersection. The MS was progressing slowly; but Joey was coping, and did so for the next 24 years.

We dealt with a stair elevator, and eventually moved our bed to the dining room after her legs were affected. There was a steady parade of Visiting Nurses. A highlight for Joey was her "Window on the World," a beautiful window in her room, which gave her a view of our yard and all outdoors.

This led to the dictating of three books reflecting Joey's ability to observe nature, to see the positive side of life, as well as her own physical situation. Her books contained colorful descriptions of her world and the family, all of which seemed to be what kept her positive attitude alive until the end. These three books, *A Different Point of View*, *Joey's Work*, and *Thoughts by Joey*, were published by Peter Randall of Portsmouth, N.H., and printed by Jim Stewart at Capitol Offset Company in Concord. Sally Chase, Joey's friend from Saint Paul's School, created the illustrations for the books. *The Concord Monitor* newspaper became interested in Joey's situation; and many feature articles and letters to the editor appeared to make her a "cause celebre" in the community. Joey had become a local folk hero, which supported her strong urge to help others in the same plight. She became a bright light for many people, in spite of her difficult illness.

A strong will and great intellect, facing forcefully ahead, helped her along the path. Joey felt strongly that persons with chronic illnesses should stay at home and out of nursing homes, if possible. A direct, but gentle letter was dictated by Joey to Barbara Bush, wife of President George H.W. Bush, and sent to the White House with a copy of Joey's book. She received a handwritten note of thanks and interest from Mrs. Bush, and continued to correspond with her. Such was Joey's willpower. The definite trend toward more home care had started.

Many family experiences followed our settlement in Concord. A family trip to California and British Columbia, and two weeks in the LaHave Islands of Nova Scotia with the Brian Johnson family was great fun. We also had an expedition with the kids to Bermuda, where Joey and I had first met in 1956. All of our children loved their visits to Cliff Island, Maine, in mid-Casco Bay. When my mother Helen died, we inherited

Treetops, her little cottage near the ferry dock, with my older brother, Grove. Later, we began spending more summer time on the island. As time progressed, and grandchildren appeared, everyone wanted to be on Cliff Island, including Joey. She loved the quietness and beauty of the place. With the help of Sue Lewis, and the use of neighbor Mike O'Reilly's Hoya lift, we were able to transport Joey to and from the house. John Keach, a friend from Concord, donated a used golf cart from the city course to be the first of many carts now on the island. This greatly widened Joey's scope and interests. In 1971, we owned Banshee, our 22-foot sailboat, which provided some exciting sails for her around the bay. Joey was hoisted down into the cockpit, well pillowed in, fully enjoying wind and ocean for the afternoon.

Our children attended St. Paul's School for the final years of their high school period. This experience was a win-win situation for them all. They have maintained friendships from both Concord High and St. Paul's throughout their lives. At age 15, our son Ben took a summer construction job at the St. Paul's infirmary and was catapulted off the fourth floor roof from failure of a faulty pulley system. Ben suffered ten long bone fractures, but miraculously no head or spinal injuries. He was in Concord Hospital for 10 weeks, cared for by the great orthopedist, Dr. Preston Clark. Ben entered private school that fall in full-length leg casts, and was able to play varsity hockey the following year. Joey and I always considered this as one of the great miracles of our lives.

My medical office provided care for St. Paul's students, giving us part faculty status at the school. We considered our faculty and sports associations there to be a major addition to our Concord lives.

As the multiple sclerosis progressed, sister Molly Scheu's

husband Ed donated a marvelous wheelchair van with a hydraulic wheelchair lift, which mobilized Joey considerably. This generous gift will never be forgotten; and after her death in 1994, the van was gifted to another MS patient. As time progressed, and the disease became more severe, it grew obvious that I could not take proper care of Joey at home. The difficult decision of moving to a nursing home was made with Joey saying that she didn't agree with it, but understood the reasons. She was to be at Mckerley's in Concord for nine years. During that time, I was able to bring her home, in the van, several times a week for dinner, which kept her partially in touch with home base. We were always so grateful for that van, which made over 1,400 round-trip dinner runs over nine years. I seemed to frequently be late, returning Joey to the nursing home after the doors were locked; but the janitor slipped me the door combination, which saved the day.

My office practice and hospital surgery were a gratifying part of life. I loved the movement between these two places, and the patients and colleagues that I came to know over the years. I was able to coax the Ob-Gyn department at the Dartmouth Medical School into sending two third-year students to us in Concord, for their six-week specialty rotations. Interaction with the students for 29 years was a special privilege and real highlight. I found after retirement that I missed these young people and the patients more than anything else. Time marches on. I stopped obstetrical care in my practice in 1980, and did only office and operative gynecology, which kept me very busy — with less night work —until my retirement on October 3, 1997.

We were always subject to great birthday and dinner parties, before Joey moved to the health facility, but afterwards as well. I guess that I was a spur-of-the-moment inviter, for I would assemble an interesting group at the last minute and go down the list if someone couldn't accept. Joey and I enjoyed these gatherings immensely. Our three children were experts at planning surprise birthdays and other events. I will never forget my 40th celebration in an upstairs dining room at the old Abbot House Restaurant on Main Street, which Joey engineered in 1970. It was a hoot, with my brothers, sister, and dear friends. All unexpected. Then there was the 60th surprise in the Westbourne living room on a Sunday morning after tennis, which I attended in my shorts and sweaty shirt. Mike and Louise O'Reilly had driven down from Cliff Island; Dick Aiken from Cape Cod; and Aunt Alice Agnew from Dorset, Vermont. The George Tracys and Warren Eberharts, among others, were in attendance. Huge fun.

Then along came the 70th surprise on Cliff Island, with 50 relatives and close pals — all planned by the kids and Judy Harris — to include a lobster and fresh corn feast in the Association Hall. Paul MacVane, our Cliff Island neighbor and friend, sat at a front table with surprise guest, Joe Perham, my favorite Maine humorist from West Paris, Maine. Joe gave a hilarious, dialectic rush of Maine humor, to which the rest of our island friends were invited. We devoured ice cream and a huge Cliff Island-shaped birthday cake.

The next extravaganza, also a complete surprise, came five years later, in 2005. It all unfolded at DiMillo's Wharf in Portland, for my 75th year, with my children, grandchildren, my brother and sister, and of course, Judy, Dick and Meghann Harris. We set sail for a three-hour sunny, Casco Bay cruise on Palawan VII, dining on my son Ben's lobster sandwiches and greenies. There were 20 of us on board, and it was a lifetime memory, again made all the better with everyone present and healthy. We all were presented with t-shirts with "BEP HAS REACHED HIS STRIDE AT 75," splashed over the front. Judy was again instrumental in coordinating all of these parties with my three children, which made the day so much fun.

Throughout Joey's three published books was a running commentary as each of our three children left for St. Paul's School, then Princeton and Dartmouth College. She and I missed them so much. We finally were "empty nesters," but Judy Harris and her daughter, Meghann were with us through so many toils. They were a bright light on the horizon and loved by both Joey and me. During the nine nursing home years, Judy was a great companion and helped the ship stay afloat at home. Joey appreciated this as much as I did. I enjoyed two dinners each week at Judy's house on Palm Street after visiting with Joey following office hours.

Her condition wound downhill from this point on, but the smile was still always there, and the indomitable spirit remained. Joey intended to complete a children's book, and though several pieces were written before her death, the book was never completed or published.

We will never forget her 12 days in the Concord Hospital Intensive Care Unit with aspiration pneumonia; but back to Mckerley's she went, with nasal oxygen for the first time in the nursing home's history. The Respiratory Care Department at our hospital took great pride in teaching staff at Mckerley's Nursing Home the tricks and technique of oxygen therapy. There was also a voice vibrator for lack of speech, and later a tracheotomy for oxygen, and a gastric tube for nourishment. Through these days, faithful friends continued to visit; and Joey was always a favorite of the health facility staff.

The final day was December 16, 1994, when Joey slipped peacefully away. Our minister, David Jones, from St. Paul's Church, immediately joined me in her room for prayers and a review of an important life, while I called all of our children. The pluck and courage had remained sturdily until the end. Joey's memorial service occurred on December 22, 1994, at our church, with a standing-room-only crowd. Joey had touched the lives of many people during her years in New Hampshire. David did a powerful job at the service.

Our three children carried the rest of the service with wonderful material, which they had prepared in the Concord library the day before. I read passages from Joey's third book. In a way, it was a mixed joyous and sad occasion to celebrate such a great life. We all met afterward, in the church's Ordway Hall, for a good luncheon and many stories. A quiet place was found in the Milleville cemetery with a large New Hampshire granite headstone dug up from Joey's flower garden on 31 Westbourne Road. Truly, it was the end of a great person and era.

Our family home was sold in November of 1997, thus ending 31 years of what I had always hoped would be a long-standing family headquarters. It was that.

Boundless *Banshee*

In June of 1971, I traveled to Stamford, Connecticut, to inspect a demo model of the 22-foot cruising rig, a Sparkman and Stephens designed Sailmaster sloop. I had looked for ages for a small, but seaworthy, sailboat to sail along the Maine coast. The idea for the Sailmaster came from "Blueberry," our friend Dick Aiken's day sailor model, which was heavy with a full lead keel and centerboard throughkeel.

The boat I looked at was built in Rotterdam, Holland, and displaced close to 3,600 pounds. The boat drew 2.5 feet with the centerboard up, and 5 feet with it down – perfect for beaching, if necessary, or for shoal water sailing. She was just what we were looking for; and we named her "Banshee" after the R-Class, John Alden designed sloop my father had sailed on Lake Erie in the 1920s.

The Banshee had four berths below — two quarter berths, and two vee berths forward. It carried a through and through head, and a sink with storage lockers. It was the perfect boat for inshore sailing. The outboard was enclosed in the well with room for two 6-gallon gas cans, separate from the cockpit. I bought the boat for $4600.00, after a quick phone call to Paul in Buffalo, New York, to see if he wanted to be a co-owner. I'll always remember his quick decision to sign on.

We moved the boat in stages to Pepperrell Cove in Kittery Point, Maine. We later purchased our own mooring, which I am still using. The first lap was from Stamford to Point Judith, Rhode Island, with the help of Paul and Dick Aiken. The same crew then journeyed through the Cape Cod Canal to Scituate, MA, each lap done on successive weekends. Finally, we sailed across Boston Harbor, with all the traffic, and into Manchester, MA. It was there that my cousin Harry Holcomb joined the party, and Aiken went home.

We continued through the Anasquam River to Newburyport Harbor, where Georgia and John Pendleton joined us. Leaving Newburyport, with the current of the Merrimack River against a flood tide, through a narrow breakwater into a dense foggy ocean, proved to be a Nantucket sleigh ride. The compass course brought us directly to Whaleback Lighthouse in Portsmouth Harbor, after having seen nothing but each other along the New Hampshire coast. We were relieved and excited to be on a mooring in Pepperrell Cove. Hooray! Our ownership of the Banshee would last 37 years and span four generations of Potters.

Our mooring in Kittery Point was purchased for $125 from Frank Frisbee, Sr., then the mooring man. It included block, chain, and buoy with pennant. We commuted from Concord for sailing. Each spring, we would sail the 50 miles east to Cliff Island. It was the custom to stop halfway and spend the night in Kennebunkport. Paul and I often did this together, but sons John Paul and Ben did their share – as did Judy, in all manner of weather.

One cold, rainy Sunday night in Kennebunkport, Paul drifted away after I bounced onto the Banshee and the dinghy tipped him out. Poor Paul, in all his foul weather gear, drifted away with the flood tide and the two oars disappeared into the darkness. Paul grabbed the bowsprit stay of a Friendship Sloop as he floated by, while calling out for someone to rescue him. I couldn't see or hear him, but a nearby boat owner could, as he made love in his own cabin. He jumped into his dinghy – pantless and with only a terrycloth shirt — and delivered Paul back aboard the Banshee, shaking with cold.

Brother Grove also helped move the boat to Casco Bay. One rainy night, Grove had bladder obstruction, and everything ashore was closed. With the help of the ship's catheter, and a tube of Crest toothpaste as a lubricant, Grove relieved his problem up on deck in the dark, while insisting that I stay below in the cabin.

Many memorable experiences occurred during these sails, including a rough passage with Judy, in a strong southwest wind, when she was new to the boat. We were clawing our way around Cape Arundel with short tacks when Judy's thumb became entangled in the jib sheet and winch. To this day, she has NO feeling in the thumb tip.

My mother, Helen Potter, loved sailing in Casco Bay. She enjoyed lying flat on the engine cover and having her picture taken. I have recently seen her comments in the "guest book" that we kept on the boat. Joey Potter, who had long-term Multiple Sclerosis, also got a big bang out of short sails while lying on cushions on the cockpit floor. This required the boys to roll her wheelchair down the ramp to the float, and manually lift her over the safety lines and down to the cockpit. It was exciting to see her big smiles as the boat heeled and she shouted for more wind. Joey loved Cliff Island and all that went with it.

We three Potter boys — Grove, Paul, and Ben - made an annual tradition of sailing 17 miles to the east of Cliff Island — to Harbor Island and Sebasco Estates, near Small Point, where we would grab a mooring and enjoy the dinner and breakfast amenities before starting back to the island. It was fun being the smallest boat in the harbor beside the maxi cruisers, which were always there. Some years, if there were time to spare, we'd cruise farther east — stopping overnight at the favorite harbors of Christmas Cove and the Coveside Marina, with owner Mike Mitchill; or Tenants Harbor and the East Wind Inn, with Manager Tim Watts and the morning blueberry pancakes. One year, we sailed down to Swans Island, and eventually to Southwest Harbor, where we moored at Steve and Dick Homers' anchorage. Dick and Kim Harris introduced us to the Homers, as they rented a Homer cottage every summer while operating their gift store in Bar Harbor. Visitors at the Homer float were always curious as to the absence of GPS and radar on our little sloop. We preferred plotting courses and following the compass.

We always searched out a decent restaurant for dinner after a long day of sailing. On these cruises, Paul slept in while Grove and I rowed ashore to search out a big breakfast, fill our coffee thermos, and row back to rout Paul out for the day's sail. It was three men in a tub, but a pretty classy tub at that. These experiences on Banshee will never be forgotten.

My sons John and Ben also enjoyed their time aboard the boat, and would often sail down or back to Kittery Point from Cliff Island. I can remember once cutting across the forbidden water in front of George H.W. Bush's house in Kennebunkport when he was in residence. The Coast Guard crash boat chased us back into bounds, away from the Bush's house.

One morning in Kennebunkport Harbor, George Bush came alongside Banshee while John was fussing below deck. President Bush complemented me on a beautiful boat as I banged on the deck with my foot, trying to reach John below. The Bush boat departed, as John emerged topsides to wonder about the deck pounding. I just said I thought he might like to meet his President. It was "Ha, Ha," and "Gee, Dad" after that.

John, Ben, and Heather definitely developed a love for the ocean and boats from their experiences aboard Banshee and on Cliff Island. From early ages, they helped me paint the bottom and prepare the boat. Heather and Dave McClelland, and their family, also enjoyed their time on board over the years.

The fourth generation children had wonderful learning sails at Cliff Island, which made me very, very happy. After marriage and a family, John went on to buy a Seasprite, 28-foot sloop, with his childhood pal, Johnny Pendleton. It was named "Flying Goose."

Upon moving to Yarmouth, Maine, with family and work, my son Ben owned the "Tiddly Idley," a small Eastern lobster boat. The Ben Potters outgrew this boat, and now own a 22-foot Eastern lobster boat, with all the bells and whistles. They commute to their neat house on Cliff Island and lobster fish with eight-year-old Sam. I have a feeling that perhaps it all started with Banshee.

During the years of our Banshee ownership, my brother Paul assumed most of the major expenses of storing and upkeep. His ideas for improvement as we progressed were always successful; and Paul was generous beyond reason. There were new lifelines, a newly built wooden hollow mast, a jell coat hull job... all major endeavors and Paul did it all. Paul and I owned the boat for many years. Then Grove became a partner. Later, my son Ben joined when Grove retired his interests.

In 2008, all owners agreed that it was time to divest the boat. Each of us had a motorboat; and sailing time was reduced. The decision was made to donate Banshee to the Maine Island Trail Association – complete with a new GPS and all equipment aboard.

It was like losing a family member. I remember Olin Stephens saying that he remembered designing the boat in 1963; and that it was one of his favorite small hulls. He also stated, that as he got older [he died at age 100] he realized that the fun in sailing was inversely proportional to the length of the boat. This was some statement from a man who designed the 130-foot Ranger, the America's Cup J-boat in 1930.

We can only be thankful we have enjoyed this marvelous boat for so long. How lucky can a family be? There is a beginning and an end to everything; and our end had come with our little Banshee. Silly to recall, I kissed her on the transom when I said good-bye.

Banshee

My 80th birthday party, Cliff Island.

Potter Grandchildren, 80th birthday:
L-R: Sam, Katie, Ariel, Ben, Simon, Izabel, Hannah, and Robin

A Bright Light Ahead:
Marriage to Judith Harris Potter
November 25, 1995

After 37 years of marriage with Joey, and her death on December 16, 1994, I planned to stay at 31 Westbourne Rd., in Concord, New Hampshire, where the Ben Potters had lived for thirty-one years, and which had been the center of our universe. Judy Harris, a young widow and wonderful person from St. Paul's School in Concord, who Joey and I had both known for many years, held a very special meaning in the Potter family. Judy and I became engaged and both retired from our working lives. Judy, as a newspaper librarian for the local Concord Monitor, Concord NH, and I; well, I think you know the answer to that. We soon began to look for another home of our own, which required selling Westbourne Road. We scoured Concord, but when Judy said, "Why don't we settle in Kittery Point, Maine?" We did just that and never regretted it for a second.

We hoped that Dick Aiken, an episcopal minister and an old friend when he taught religion at St. Paul's, would marry us. He lived in Truro on Cape Cod, so the wedding was planned for tiny St. Mary of the Harbor, an Episcopal church in Provincetown on the outer Cape. We invited 40 family and close friends; and the ceremony occurred at 4:00 p.m. on a stormy Saturday, November 25, 1995. We all arrived in the downpour, and the wedding couldn't have been more beautiful, simple, and good.

A small bouquet sat on the altar, with a burning candle in memory of Joey Potter and Ron Harris, Judy's first husband, who had died unexpectedly of a spontaneous stroke in 1983 at age 43. Ron had been the trainer for all the athletic teams at St. Paul's and also managed the school's infirmary.

My new bride-to-be arrived with me at the church in her lacy white dress, and hair band to match, a thing of beauty. I walked Judy down the short aisle with lovely music from the little church organ, and the wedding began. Dick and George Wells, St. Mary's Rector, married us with a short and simple ceremony; and we are now together for always. We dashed through the rain to the old Red Inn nearby in Provincetown. The fireplace was flickering, and a Christmas tree was decorated, though Judy had brought Thanksgiving decorations for each table.

The reception included our combined five children — Heather, Ben, John Paul, and Dick and Meghann Harris – and their spouses. First grandchild, Hannah Rose Potter, was with us as a beautiful young toddler; so the gang was all there, and it seemed so natural and fun. The wedding toasts and speeches were all-inclusive with laughs and wild stories. Our roast beef dinner concluded with cake cutting, poems, and more toasts, which Judy and I will not forget. We settled into an upstairs room at the Inn overlooking Cape Cod Bay for the night; and the day was complete

Three Cheers! A new life had begun for us both, now with nine grandchildren, good health, and an interesting life and retirement on the Maine coast.

The morning after, we had a happy, informal brunch at

Betsy and John Pendleton's house high on a windy, Truro bluff beside Cape Cod Bay. We traveled "overseas" to Martha's Vineyard, for a special honeymoon at the Daggett House on Edgartown Harbor. We have returned to the Vineyard every November to celebrate our anniversary.

On looking back after these years of a second marriage for Judy and me, I realize how important that Cape Cod ceremony was for us both. I have relished our lives together with new friends, neighbors, ocean and boats at our doorstep. Most of all, our families are within a few hours driving distance, enabling us to be a part of the grandchildren's birthdays, school and sports activities, and individual development. Thank goodness for all of them.

Judy and Ben's Wedding
November 25, 1995

Judy's daughter Meghann and son Dick

Wedding Cruise in Maine
L-R: Molly and Ed Scheu, Judy and Ben

*Judy's 50th High School Reunion
West Haven, Connecticut*

Judy with our grandkids, Henry and Eliza

Brother Grove Potter Memories
Notes from Westminster Church Funeral Service, Buffalo, New York
ೞ೮

Thank you all for coming today to celebrate the life of a very special person.

Grove was the sixth direct generation of Potter physicians, starting with Benjamin E. Potter, who was born in South Dartmouth, Massachusetts, in 1789, the year that our Constitution was signed. Benjamin E. Potter settled in Western New York to practice medicine on the frontier, and to fight in the War of 1812. Our grandfather, Irving White Potter, obstetrician extraordinaire, delivered his grandchildren, including Grove, as breech babies, by internal podalic version.

Brother Paul and Grove assisted Grandfather Potter and our dad, Milton G. Potter, in their practices here in Buffalo, until their last years. Grove and Paul then embarked on a dual practice of Obstetrics and Gynecology in this city. For 40 years, it was a close and flawless practice. Paul and Grove thought, practiced, and sounded exactly alike on the telephone. Patients could not tell the voices apart. Grove and Paul had both trained at Bellevue Hospital in New York City, with their old friend, chief, and mentor, Gordon Watkins Douglas. These two brothers had a "hands-on" training at Bellevue, and were very clever and innovative, both surgically and medically. Sister Molly and I were the black sheep of the family who migrated to New England.

As Grove retired from practice, he and Lorene assumed a whole new career as ship's doctor and Episcopal assistant. They completed 75 voyages over ten years to all corners of the Earth, including Antarctica. Wow. What an avocation! This couple loved to travel, and they were good at it.

Growing up in Buffalo, I remember Grove as a hellion at home. He would attempt impossible projects late at night, such as bringing a huge, round Gulf Oil sign around a curving staircase, and up to his second-floor bedroom in our apartment on Norwood Avenue.

He and Lorene merged into a fine team as life progressed. They relied on each other for so much – Grove more so than Lorene. Their family of four children and 10 grandchildren always came first…babysitting in San Francisco or wherever. You name it, they were there. Nothing seemed to be too much effort. It was a puzzle that came together. They were truly life partners for over 50 years.

As a family, we enjoyed Grove and his family so often and so well – whether a home visit in Maine, or a barge trip on the English canals. There were also many medical conference trips we attended together over the years, which always worked well.

Grove had some great and interesting quirks. He loved to make and eat huge breakfasts: cereal, followed by fried eggs, sunny-side up over pancakes, with bacon, coffee, and orange juice.

His long-distance telephone conversations were another example. Grove became uneasy if we talked too long, even though it was often on "my nickel," and occasionally on his.

We consulted medically often, which was a big advantage for me. I will miss these random long-distance talks, which usually ended with a joke.

Grove was the quintessentially well-rounded physician and human being. He combined the new and the old arts and sciences of medicine and of life. What a combination!

All of us here salute him for all he stood for – his love, humor, and innate smarts. God bless our brother, husband, father, grandfather, uncle, and friend, Grove Potter.

Retirement 101: Kittery Point, Maine
ଓଞ୍ଚ

Retirement surprises are never ending. In September 2006, I joined a group of retired men and women, in a group known as the York Maine Hospital Transportation. Our job was to transport patients to and from their doctors' appointments and York Hospital-related activities. This is a free service to patients, which is unheard of in my experience. The service allows mostly elderly people, many of whom are no longer driving, to reach their designated appointments – and therefore keep the hospital's level of business higher than it might otherwise be – a super marketing venture.

The group of eleven drivers, who operated six hospital-owned cars, was a closely-knit group of interesting retired people. They seemed to care about each other, and regularly helped the newer drivers, in even small ways. This group was spearheaded by our dispatcher, Charlie White, retired himself, and one of the fairest people on earth. Always kind and polite, and stationed in the hospital Transportation Office, Charlie planned our routes for the following day, and called us per-diem drivers the night before to confirm. I averaged two to three, four- to eight-hour driving days each week, and had the option to decline work if other things were happening in my life…a nice option of the per-diem driver status. The other full-time drivers were committed to specific days and expected to be there. Our compensation was $11.00 per hour.

For me, the attraction of this new job was the passengers themselves. Most were women in their seventies and eighties, but there were some men and younger souls, too. Many lived alone in low-income housing, and may not have talked with anyone for weeks. So in the car, the conversation came pouring out in so many ways – happy, sad, funny, and boring...quite a variation usually.

One sees firsthand how hard it is for many people to live and survive with their problems – physical, familial, and financial. My profit from this work was the association with the group who continued to see their life situations positively and good naturedly.

One older lady said to me, "Want to hear about my three husbands?"

When I replied, "How are they all?" she responded with a wink, "They were all drunks, and they are all dead."

I tried not to laugh in these situations, but continued to drive. I didn't reveal my past physician life, but if asked, I did tell the truth. The patients were most appreciative of the hospital service, and told us so, even with the occasional "tip," which I turned over to York Hospital. We covered much of Southern Main in our travels – Kittery, the Berwicks, Eliot, York, Ogunquit, Wells, and Kennebunk.

My traveling companions often reminded me of the mix of daily office patients in my medical practice, with a combination of their daily problems, which I did not attempt to "treat" on the road.

Two Important People
೧೪೮೦

Important people make a difference in one's life. Two men, among others, played important roles in my life: Charles Ricker of Cliff Island, Maine, and Olin Stephens of New York City, and Hanover, New Hampshire.

Charles Ricker was born on Chebeague Island, Maine, into a family of fishermen. He moved to Cliff Island in mid-life, becoming a longstanding lobster catcher until his death in 1957. My family and I began our summers on this island in 1939. I was nine years old, and my brother Paul was seven. At this writing, in 2009, 70 years have passed.

I had a habit of hanging around the waterfront, listening to the wild stories the fishermen told while sitting around the fish houses and smoking. One of these men was Charles Ricker, then in his early 70s. Everything important seemed to happen early in the morning; and I was an early riser. Soon I was eating breakfast in the Ricker's kitchen; and before long I had become a young sternman on Mr. Ricker's lobster boat. He had always been a solo fisherman, but out of great kindness, he took me aboard at $1.00 per day. We left the mooring at 6:00 a.m., and were usually back by 1:00 p.m., having had "lunch" at about 10:00 a.m.

This man was very kind to me as a young boy. We talked

and laughed easily, despite the great age difference. Charles Ricker smoked Everyday plug tobacco in his pipe, chipping it off with a jack knife. I do think that this influenced my pipe smoking, which started at age 19, and has lasted 60 years and counting.

During our hours on the boat, I heard stories about his swordfishing as a young man, and many yarns about sardining along the Maine coast. This man had a twinkle in his eye most of the time; but when the occasion arose – luckily infrequently –he also had a huge temper. He taught me to swear when necessary, which has stood me in good stead.

Once a week, we would travel to Portland for lobster bait and groceries. This was during World War II, when the inner Long Island harbor was the headquarters of the North Atlantic Fleet. Battleships, including the "Missouri" battleship, cruisers, and destroyers, traveled in and out through Hussey Sound. The local fisherman needed huge identifying numbers on their hulls, and multicolored flags flying for the same reason, as we passed through the steel nets between Pumpkin Knob and Peaks Island. In town, after doing the chores, Charles Ricker would stop at the bar for a glass of beer. I would sit on a stool, drinking a Pepsi, listening to the drunks whoop it up. We always left for the island after one beer. These days stand out in vivid color, never to be forgotten. Charles Ricker was a surrogate grandfather who influenced me in so many ways. Even today, I find that some of my habits date back to watching Charles Ricker proceed through his day.

ଓଞ୍ଜ

Two Important People

Another important person in my life, who I greatly admired, was Olin Stephens II. I only knew him for perhaps 10 years after meeting him at my sister Molly Scheu's dinner party in Hanover. Olin was a preeminent, world-class yacht designer who had started his career in his 20s with his brother, Rod Stephens. They were personally close and worked well together. Olin Stephens was a versatile artist when designing the Lightning Class racing daysailer, as well as the huge 120-foot J Class Ranger for the America's Cup challenge in the 1930s.

This man was retired when we met. He was the most friendly and unassuming man I had met in ages. I took it upon myself to invite him to a Concord Yacht Club dinner, and drove to Hanover to pick him up. He enjoyed himself so much at these meetings that we made him an honorary member of our yacht club. He returned each December for six or seven years, until the effort became too great. I got to know this man through his openness, and his overnights at our house in Concord after each yacht club dinner, until Judy and I retired and moved to Kittery Point.

Olin's stories were classics, though they took some drawing out. I heard many during our breakfasts alone in my house. In his early 20s, Olin and his brother sailed their fifty-foot yawl, Dorade, across the Atlantic and won the Trans-Atlantic race. Upon reaching England, the brothers anchored in the dark, and awoke in the morning beside King George V's royal yacht Britannia. The King invited the boys aboard for tea. Olin told me that the old king was courtly, but very friendly, and congratulated them heartily. These wonderful stories fascinated me — although taking a little priming to hear.

I told Olin Stephens that he would be one of my mentors, and he said that he had never been a mentor before. He was quite surprised. He was constantly traveling the world to either races or launchings of his restored, great old racing boats. As the grand old man of yacht racing, Olin wouldn't refuse an invitation to any occasion; and he never seemed to tire of travel throughout the world. He would arrive at our house with his pajamas and toothbrush, and seem perfectly happy and relaxed. He missed his wife Suzie so much – she had died after they moved to Vermont from Scarsdale in retirement.

Olin seemed to enjoy hearing about our Sailmaster sloop, Banshee, which he designed in 1963, and which we sailed for 37 years with four generations of Potters aboard over the seasons since 1971. Olin claimed it was one of his favorite small hulls to come off his board. The greatest line I ever heard from this guy was when he claimed that in his old age he had concluded that the pleasure in sailing was inversely proportional to the length of the boat. He didn't agree with, or like, the light displacement sailing yachts of today, which placed speed ahead of safety and comfort at sea.

The sincerity and wisdom this man mixed with a tinge of wry humor was something to behold. In 2008, Olin Stephens died at age 100. I asked him during a visit before his death what it felt like to be a centenarian. His response: "What is a centenarian?" End of story. Such a person lived the full and productive life.

Two Important People

Olin Stephens at the Concord Yacht Club being inducted as an honorary member of Snowshoe Club, Concord, NH

Charles Ricker and Ben Potter in Lobster Boat Cliff Island, Maine 1944

Brother Paul Potter's 70th Birthday Toast:
January 23, 2003
Harvard Club – Boston, Massachusetts
୧ଓ୭୦

Dear Paul,

First, a happy and healthy birthday this year, and years to come. You will probably outlive all of us if you continue to wear the raincoat and rubbers in Buffalo all winter.

What about a few flashbacks on these years? You won't forget Hodge Avenue, where we all started with the playhouse – the big snow slide off its roof – and the enormous cherry tree. How about Miss "Yoo-Who" Hill next door, who used to take our slingshot spitballs into her newspaper while reading by the window? Mrs. Martin on the other side; and yes, Miss Ruckle and Miss Brown, the Bobbsey Twins across the street who, at age 85, would speed off to church every week in their Model-T Ford roadster. Mother herded us to unpleasant visits with Dr. Garrotsen, the dentist, who drilled teeth with less-than-usual anesthesia. Then there were Lizzy and Buddy Graham, whose mother could scarcely get above a whisper when calling her children in for lunch with her whiskey voice.

There was 35-cent Charlie, the barber on Bryant Street, who snipped off part of brother Grove's earlobe, and kept a phantom monkey [which we never saw] in the basement. There was Smither's soda fountain with five-cent ice cream cones with jimmies. I could never remember what we did with the empty spools collected from Alexander the tailor on Hodge Ave. Oh, well.

Do you remember freezing to death at Well's Skating Rink up the street? The garage where we put on our skates with the wood stove that was never hot; and bald Mr. Wells would laugh and throw on more wet wood. There was Aunt Ada, and Marion Tanner, the aunt of playwright Patrick Dennis, who had used her as the model for "Auntie Mame" of Broadway fame. Marion Tanner lived around the corner on Ashland Avenue. These ladies were both memorable characters, and so kind to all of us.

The great amount of time spent at the Himmelsbach grandparents' home on Elmwood Avenue was impressive during the Buffalo years. They were like surrogate parents. Coleman's Ginger Ale was always in the refrigerator; and our grandmother's homemade-spiced pears were in the fruit cellar. Much to Nonna's consternation, Gertrude, the cook, always licked her fingers while serving food in the dining room. Our grandparents were always generous to the men looking for employment during hard times. The men would be given "food for work" on the back steps; but they were never turned away. The Himmelbachs were your quintessential caring grandparents, who loved each other, and all of us. Outward emotion was rarely shown, but Grandpa often patted Nonna's cheek from behind her chair after dinner – never a kiss.

I remember how happy Grampa was to drive us to Lackawanna Railroad Station to watch the steam engines arrive and depart. Also, it pleased him for all of us to board

Brother Paul Potter's 70th Birthday Toast

the Niagara River ferry in Buffalo, and ride round-trip to Fort Erie in Canada, for a nickel each way. I think this trip must have reminded him of his many schooner voyages as a young doctor, bringing workers to Boston from Africa and the Azores.

It was always a treat to eat meals at their house. Grampa George would pretend to do the breaststroke at the table when we put too much maple syrup on our "fried mush." He would often hold his head at dinner; and Nonna would say, "Your grandfather is very tired," – even when diminutive Mr. Gibbs, Grampa's lawyer, was there for the evening, which he often was. Merton Gibbs was so short and frail that his feet never touched the floor. I often wondered what those two men talked about closeted in the medical office after dinner.

We frequently had lunch with our grandparents, Irving and Grace Potter, at 186 Chapin Parkway. These were usually medical case discussions with our dad, and Hugh and Bob McDowell, all obstetricians, with Grampa Potter leading them on. Grandma Potter was usually silent, shifting all her pill bottles around, almost oblivious to her surroundings. Margaret, the maid, endlessly circled the table, bringing more food from the kitchen. I remember Sunday noon lunches with Grampa Potter at Newton's Restaurant, on Delaware Avenue at Bryant Street. Grampa always said that good food was not a waste of money. These were caring, good people, who loved their young people and influenced us in so many ways.

We got our medical start as teenagers, at the Millard Filmore Hospital, where we watched obstetrical births from stools in the operating room. We were there at the invitation of Father and Grandfather; and we often brought friends along after school. What a contrast to the present day!

After many apartment moves in Buffalo, where the rent was raised each time, it was off to Greenfield, Mass., and Montclair,

New Jersey, where we lived in the apartment over Uncle Hobey Agnew's medical office. We both attended Hillside Middle School and Montclair High, where you were a much better student and athlete than I. Sixty-five years later, I am still in touch with Craig Hibben, my best New Jersey friend. The Agnews looked after us well, with cousin George and Drika, who seemed much younger than us during those years.

A major part of life began in 1939, at Cliff Island, Maine. Mother left a great legacy for the family, which has thus far included four generations. Our famous lobster and fish business was our strength while the professional fishermen were fighting in World War II. We were too young to enlist. We started with a wooden rowboat and outboard, and a few second-hand lobster traps. I fished; and you sold the product to the summer people. I later became sternman on Charles Ricker's bigger lobster boat, with bigger catches and more profit.

Life became more complicated when we both left for Phillips Andover, and our respective colleges, but sure enough, we regrouped at McGill Medical School and shared an apartment in Montreal during my last two years of graduate school. Then it was on to Ob-Gyn residencies and medical practice, in Buffalo and Concord, NH, for me.

These were all good, though not always easy years. You and I have been lucky brothers to have done so many things together, and still be going strong. All of this has meant a lot to me.

These are a few memories that will encourage more of your own. Stay well; and HAPPY BIRTHDAY today.

Read by me to my brother Paul, and the family attending, at the Harvard Club in Boston, Mass.

Lobsters Are the Bee's Knees:
A Talk with my McGill Medical School Class, 50th Reunion, Montreal, Canada
October 2007

ೞಙ

Knowing that most of us are already retired from medical careers, I am here to advertise and promote retirement as a third chapter of our lives. The first segment is that of growing up with education; the second is family and professional years; and the third retirement. If possible, retirement is not to be missed.

A senior internist and partner of mine taught that retirement had to be trained and prepared for two to three years before the actual event. He did this himself with such grace and productivity that I have tried to emulate him.

I found that there were so many activities of interest that I had not had time for during a busy 35-year Ob-Gyn practice, that the retirement choices were easy to make.

Having married wonderful Judy — after my first wife, Joey, had died in 1994, after twenty-four years with Multiple Sclerosis — we bought an old house in the tiny seaside village of Kittery Point, Maine. Both of us had hoped to live by the ocean at some point. After rebuilding this dilapidated old house, we moved into the perfect spot – complete with a small woodworking shop in the basement, blasted out of rock. Life can be beautiful.

I immediately applied for a non-commercial Maine lobster fishing license and found a small used lobster fishing boat, the "Kittery Belle." I haul my traps, weather dependent, several times weekly; and though the lobsters have become scarcer in recent years, I seem to catch my share. I enjoy being on the water, usually alone, with safety measures of a VHF radio, a cell phone, and a life jacket.

Another great love is honey bee keeping. I keep three hives behind our garage. The delicious end product is bottled, and delivered with red ribbons at Christmastime. A honey bee colony is a magical matriarchal mystery, which is great fun to work with and to watch develop. Each of the 50,000 female worker bees in each hive flies three miles a day to fetch pollen and nectar for the colony. The foraging bees pollinate our flowers and crops; and provide food for the queen bee, the few hundred lazy, male drone bees, and the thousands of developing offspring growing from the 1,200 eggs the single queen bee lays each day.

I have had some important mentors in my lifetime, all of whom have influenced me considerably. Besides two sets of important grandparents who lived near us while growing up, I have followed some steps in the life of well-known yacht designer Olin Stephens, now 98 years old. He is still young at heart and unbelievably spritely. Then there is Reggie Henshaw, an eighty year English Master Bee Keeper, who leads me through the occasional thickets of raising honey bees. He separates my honey from the comb, and I trade my Maine lobsters in return. The bartering system still works in perfect balance. This man with his pixyish sense of humor has learned to accept the knocks and niceties of life with equal aplomb.

Thankfully, most of the surgical patients in my practice healed well and went home. I became interested, though, in the Hospice movement during early retirement. I joined a large group in Exeter, New Hampshire, to organize an Ethics Council to provide advice to patients, patients' families, and to the Hospice workers themselves in tricky, end-of-life situations. The council included twelve marvelous and intelligent local leaders, and took three years to mobilize and become productive.

My time spent with five children and nine grandchildren, all of whom live within easy driving distance, has trumped all other retirement activities. Judy and I attend non-stop birthday parties, school concerts, and sports events; and watch the children grow up, each with enthusiastic, differing personalities and talents. These are the perks of retirement.

෴

In short, every day counts for a lot. We in this class are at the same stage of life's career. Our health has been all important, and some have been luckier than others. An element of fun each day is so important. This fun is occasionally hard to locate, but must be invented at times using a little imagination.

The answers seem to be family, health, and interesting activities for successful retirement years. This part of life, particularly after our professional years, is not to be missed, if possible. To return to McGill, and Montreal, after 50 years is the frosting on the cake. I feel very, very lucky. I hope that you do, too.

Benjamin Potter

Ben on his lobster boat, "Kittery Belle."

Judy and I

"Old Men and the Sea"
⋄⋄⋄

Two Manolin characters lived as young boys, one fictional and the other true to life. In reading *The Old Man and the Sea* for a course on Ernest Hemingway that Judy and I audited at Southern New Hampshire University several years ago, I immediately noticed a familiar, "déjà vu" sensation from my early summers spent with another "Santiago" type in my years as a small boy on a tiny coastal Maine island. The relationships were so similar; I could not help but compare them.

Hemingway painted the most sensitive picture of devotion between Manolin and Santiago. This was not true fiction in my view, but real life itself. My personal admiration was for my mentor and teacher, Charles Ricker. Mr. Ricker was island born; uneducated in the formal sense; and a lifelong seagoing fisherman – wise beyond words. Even at age 75, when I first met him, Mr. Ricker was a man of huge strength. As with Santiago and Manolin, Captain Ricker showed me enormous caring and confidence – beginning when I was only 12 years old. He was my friend and confidant during my early, formative years, when I served as his "stern man" every day while lobster fishing. I consider those years as important as any part of my education in forming lifelong habits and philosophies.

Santiago dealt with the basic elements of his uncomplicated life — the sea, its fish, and all aspects of weather — from within his small sailing skiff. These were the ingredients of his religion and life, packaged with a warm relationship with young Manolin. Nothing else in his sphere caused worry or wearing. Food, sleep, and shelter were of secondary importance.

I, too, recognized, perhaps unconsciously, these traits in my friend on the island. His tanned and wrinkled face and arms — added to crooked fingers from fishing for swordfish and sardines in freezing winter temperatures — all seemed unimportant in his daily urge to board a small fishing boat to tend a long string of lobster traps in weather, fair or foul.

Santiago and Manolin fit together as hand in glove. I had the feeling that Charles Ricker and I did also, despite the great age difference. Certain chemistry allowed this to happen. As with Santiago, I noticed sparkling eyes, pipe in mouth, and a kindness beyond belief. No unpleasant words were ever spoken between us, and each seemed to enjoy the other's company. To a young boy this was important. In my case this may have related to the absence of a live-in father, but I can't be sure. I admired both men's confidence in stretching the safety envelope, but never too far. Each understood his abilities and limits perfectly. These tricks and traits allowed both men to reach daily goals, not always related to successful fishing.

The two fishermen lived their daily lives with memories and experiences of the past. Endless tales unwound as my friend and I hauled and baited his lobster traps around the bay. As with Santiago's great Marlin, so was Captain Ricker's story of a huge swordfish on the outer fishing banks. While landing this creature from his dory, the fish rose to the surface and pierced the bottom of the small boat with its sword, narrowly missing the fisherman's feet. Man or boy never forgets these colorful experiences.

Ernest Hemingway knew well the prototype of the character, Santiago, as I had known my friend, Charles Ricker. They are both worth remembering. The depth of Hemingway's sensitivity and tenderness reflects a quality of the author himself. I had not recognized this part of his character in any previous reading of the author's work. This has caused me to re-evaluate a complex personality. He has become more interesting and worth reading.

Fish bait, like ammunition, was a means to an end for both men. Hemingway describes many times the source and use of bait, bait, and more bait. So, too, was Captain Ricker consumed with obtaining the perfect, smelly, decomposed lobster bait. He often mentioned to me that our bait was "sweet'sa nut" so important for good lobster fishing.

Manolin and I both met our mentors in the early gray dawn for breakfast before going to sea. I at the Ricker's small but comfortable kitchen, with wood smoke pouring from the chimney, and pie and molasses cookies on the table. Manolin Santiago also led the way to hot coffee for his friend. These essentials were the glue, which bound us all together, and often predicted a good day ahead. Faceless, loud voices were heard across our cove at the island as other fisherman prepared to leave the harbor.

There was steadfastness among older men of the sea. They are often unfamiliar with the latest equipment and technology; but rarely fail to return to port in the worst of weather. Santiago improvised in so many ways — from catching life-saving fish to fashioning a backup harpoon from his own hand knife. His words — "Now is no time to think of what you do not have, but think of what you can do with what there is" — were typical of both men. They lived always for the present, never worrying about the past, or what might happen ahead. I am sure that this philosophy helped to maintain their physical and emotional strength through long lives. It has taught me a huge lesson as well.

Endurance, when called upon, can far exceed what we consider our average limits. Santiago used inner resources to endure three nights without sleep among untold dangers at hand. Charles Ricker spent many sleepless nights searching for fish known to approach the ocean surface at night, thus assuring a larger catch. Both men placed necessity ahead of comfort and ease. The human body and brain must surely function to excess when needed. Hemingway's Santiago endured lacerated and cramped fingers, which took second place to his concentration on landing the hooked marlin. Bitter winter temperatures and saltwater caused frostbitten and gnarled fingers on the New England coast.

These situational similarities and human observations drawn from my experiences contain enough lessons for a lifetime. The strengths and weaknesses of two determined men are reasons for pause and consideration. They both neutralized a hard life with the levity of baseball and a keen sense of humor. This, combined with an unspoken faith in a stronger power, saw both men through to their ends.

Later in life, I became a modest lobsterman, the result of my boyhood experiences with old Mr. Ricker. Physical and intellectual strength, combined with faith, can point in many directions, and are strong lessons to have learned. Ernest Hemingway did not lead by personal and real life example himself. His characters did it so magically for him. They provided me with a real life comparison for which I was grateful.

The Mysterious Business of Mentoring Young Boys in the Kittery, Maine Schools 2001-2008

ಔಝ

Once about a time, I volunteered at the Mitchell Elementary School to read aloud to the kindergarten and first grade classes in the school library. All of the kids sat on the rug, one class at a time, with the rabble rousers always in the back row doing something unrelated to listening. I learned that it was important to hold the book backwards, so the kids could see the pictures and the reader could only see the cover. I found that by holding the book at a cocky angle, both interests were satisfied. The children were great; and I enjoyed this a lot.

After I'd been reading to the young kids in the library for a year or so, Principal David Foster asked me to mentor two first grade boys who were having trouble settling down in school. I opted to meet with them together, rather than separately, feeling that they might be able to gain by doing our activities together — even though they were very different people. Mr. Foster was not sure this was a good idea. This started a pathway of eight years with these boys, until they entered Traip Academy in Kittery as ninth graders.

Dalton and Ben came from difficult and unsettled families, to put it mildly. Even in the first grade, their early social skills were non-existent. They were good young kids, above average in intelligence; but both were lazy to the point of not caring. I liked them both and continued to through the eight years. I respected them — and they me — throughout our time together. Fair to say that both were unsure of themselves, even at a young age; but that gradually, some confidence developed each succeeding year. Both sets of parents were eventually divorced, and never had any contact with me during my years with their boys. I had a feeling that they didn't care, and were not interested. Each year, these two guys would elect to meet again with me, of their own volition and will; so on it went. I left it up to them.

We met once weekly for an hour during school. With the help of their homeroom teachers, we coordinated an hour on a morning that I was free and went from there. We read aloud, and performed plays by reading parts from the short play scripts. We laughed a lot along the way. Sports was also a part of the program, with one boy better coordinated than the other. We built small wooden projects, which would be started and cut out in my home workshop, and timed for delivery under the Christmas tree for their parents. The boys were whizzes on the computer, even at an early age, which led to studies of the National Parks, countries, etc. At the start of school each year, the boys made a "wish list" of projects to do; and we tried to follow it. We had to practice each week to say good morning to the librarian, which was not a habit in their collection.

The lazy factor played an important part in not getting homework projects done on time; and this took constant prodding. There seemed to be no support at home to improve this situation. During our final eighth grade year together, the boys, of all things, wanted to write a play. I had

The Mysterious Business of Mentoring Young Boys

to do a bit of research with the English teacher and the computer to learn to start this gig, but it came to pass. It was decided that we would do a spoof of the "Rosie O'Donnell Show," with the camera running. Dalton played Rosie, and I was to be Albert Einstein, as guest along with Kevin Garnet, a Boston Celtics player, whose part Ben played. Other "guests" appeared on the "show," too, and we were led in discussion by "Rosie," who wore a long green wig for the occasion. The school camera ran, and there were a lot of laughs. The resulting DVD was very funny; and we three all got copies, courtesy of Shapleigh School.

The "play" ended our eight years of activities before the boys started high school. There is no way of measuring mentor activity; but one hopes that he or she can play some small part in the lives of disadvantaged kids. We came to like each other through all of this, and maybe this will make some small difference in two young lives. Yes, it was an effort to plan our activities with a little imagination involved, but I was glad to have been a part of it. Two fine boys were on their way in high school.

Both boys graduated from high school in 2013. One, who orginally had less confidence, became a star football player and was admitted as a college freshman. The second boy opted out of the application process, at least for now.

I see them now at Christmastime, and will look forward to watching their lives continue. It was fun, and fortunate, for me to have this experience during my retirement.

Marvelous "Madrigal" Memories
൱

It is with great fondness that I think back to the many, many sails I was able to join on that great yawl, Madrigal, with Rob Bass and his many special crewmen. My introduction to Concordias began 25 years ago, at a Concord Yacht Club dinner in the home of our then-Commodore, Bill Morrison. I sat at the same table as Concordia designer Ray Hunt, who was the evening's guest speaker. Soon I was invited by Rob Bass to sail with him on one of many passages from Tenants Harbor to South Dartmouth, Mass., where Madrigal would be hauled for the winter. It must be said now that Robby Bass' generosity in allowing so many of us, who were "new " friends at the time, to join him on these cruises over the years was impressive. He knew instinctively who had sailing in our systems, and was ALWAYS able to put together a perfectly balanced group of men to be together in a small space. It was uncanny. I will be forever grateful.

Robert Bass was a man of many colors, mostly bright. I first knew him to be a "sternish" lawyer at Cleveland, Waters, and Bass in Concord. I soon learned, however, that on a vessel at sea, this man would become the world's best shipmate and sailing teacher. I was never embarrassed to ask questions, and knew that I could expect a reasoned and full answer. Rob had a way of obtaining the confidence and cooperation of his crewmembers. His mastery of the Shipmate, the coal stove on Madrigal, led to the famous Bass two-wine, and roast lamb dinners. That stove was always a friend, providing hot soup and cocoa for the watchmen on chilly overnight passages. I had never sailed with a skipper who provided marked hand towels in the head for each crewman.

Regardless of our times aboard Madrigal, Robby always led a safety tour around ship for everyone to learn switches, through hulls, man overboard equipment, and anchoring procedure. Before leaving port on any passage, each of us was presented with a list of "to do's" and items to find at the grocery store. It was finely orchestrated, and a helpful procedure for us to follow on our own boats. Nothing like experience. We never left Tenants Harbor without a pail of live lobster to cook on the trip south; but the heavy steam pouring from the galley did not help any tendency toward early seasickness.

I was never so overwhelmed as when Rob Bass asked me to crew on his transatlantic voyage to Scandinavia. Never had I wanted to do anything so much; but because of family illness, I was unable. I also remember him asking me to gather a crew and sail Madrigal back to the States after one of his trips to Bermuda. That did not happen either — for the same family reason. Many years later, I was able to sail westward from Europe to Barbados as ship's doctor on a charter schooner. I never forgot those original Madrigal invitations. Bravo, Herr Capitaine!

Many memories rush by as I sit here. One pops up from Pulpit Harbor, where we anchored in a cold rain after a windy day sail around the bay, heavily heeled. Soon it was clear that we had fouled a lobster buoy. Serious discussion

Marvelous Madrigal Memories

followed as to who would dive — with a knife in the near darkness — to clear the prop. Quietly, and with nary a word, our captain appeared in his Speedo suit, and was over the side with flashlight, goggles, and knife. After re-anchoring, this sort of attitude inspired us all.

Several passages to Saint John, New Brunswick, and Mahone Bay and Halifax, Nova Scotia, stand out. A memorable dinner unfolded at the Sword and the Anchor Restaurant after the overnight passage to Nova Scotia and arrival in Mahone Bay. While driving to the ferry in Yarmouth the next morning, we learned by radio of the horror of 9/11 in New York. I could not believe my ears. We were the last ferry to enter Bar Harbor before all American ports were closed. It was a sad day for all, and the start of a new era.

We were equally impressed each time at the passage in the Saint John River over the reversing falls at slack high water. This had followed an impressive fogbound sail up the Grand Manan Channel in a flood tide with Tom Alpert and my brother Paul. Robby had stayed behind at the last minute due to a serious illness Patty Bass was being treated for at Massachusetts General Hospital. But Tom Alpert, master of all things GPS, guided us into Saint John's harbor without our ever seeing the breakwall or the Digby ferry, which chugged by at close range. Never such thick fog, ever.

On one of my last cruises with Robby, and after receiving the usual number of mailings containing detailed plans for the passage, we set sail from Rockport. After a day of good wind, and 75 miles into the Gulf of Maine, the engine refused to start. We were taking on water near the bow. I will never forget our skipper calmly calling the Rockport Marine and ordering a new $10,000 diesel engine, while sipping a hot cup of coffee in the forward cabin. This is how impressions are made. We tacked and reversed course for the marina, where Madrigal was hauled and the leak repaired while waiting for a new engine.

I am ever grateful to my friend, Rob Bass, for his thoughtfulness, kindness, and steadfast willingness to try a new course or a new idea, and teach others along the way.

Wrap Up

October 2015: I have finally finished this little book!

The opportunity to write this memoir has been a gift.

My ancestors' lives have always inspired me to move ahead in a good direction.

I have had an interesting and full life having just celebrated my 85th birthday with yet another sailing adventure, thanks to my family, around Casco Bay in Portland, Maine.

Presently, I just got back from Oslo, Norway with my brother, Paul and my two sons, Ben and John, from a Norwegian coastal steamer trip from Northern Norway to Bergen in Southern Norway.

How lucky my life has been!

My two wives, Joey and Judy have been the keys to my success, as well as my five children and nine grandchildren. All of you have given me great pleasure and so many happy days.

As I mentioned earlier, this book was written for my children and their children to help sort out a complex family. I hope that it will do its job.

Love and thanks to all,

Benjamin E Potter

The Potter boys debarking in Bergen, Norway – October 2015
L-R: Ben, Ben Sr., Paul, and John

Afterword

I am grateful for the patience and guidance of Jack Beckwith of Beckwith Books in Rye, New Hampshire. Jack edited my material prior to his death in 2012. Stephanie McSherry of Edgecomb, Maine then came to the rescue to continue in Jack's footsteps. This was a lifesaver for me.

I also want to thank my patient publisher, Tom Holbrook of RiverRun Bookstore and Piscataqua Press in Portsmouth, New Hampshire. Tom always made it easy by encouraging me through crank days while writing this memoir.

I am most thankful for the strong support of my family, especially for their technical know-how as I completed this project.

I have been lucky to have had a life filled with a loving family, a stimulating professional career, and many wonderful friends.

Benjamin Elon Potter
Kittery Point
Maine, 2015

www.ingramcontent.com/pod-product-compliance
Lightning Source LLC
Chambersburg PA
CBHW030000050426
42451CB00006B/69